S0-ARO-949

Happens All the Time

Cheating in the Good Ol' U.S.A.

STORIES BY

MARK CHAUPPETTA, PRIVATE EYE

Foreword
by Douglas Florence

The story goes that Mark Chauppetta was in sunny California trying to get his acting career started. I've seen about a million people come here with that in mind, serving pizzas and wheatgrass and waiting for their big break. But something about Mark was different – he was the kind of guy who made his own luck. On leave from the prison system in Massachusetts, where he had started college for criminal justice, he'd had it with banquet waitering and being an underwear model… so he picked up the phone and responded to an ad he had seen about my company, Itani Florence Investigations.

"I'm Mark Chauppetta," he told me straight out, "I'm a struggling actor, and I have a background in law enforcement. I've never done any investigative work before but I need a fucking job."

I happened to be in a jam, needing a co-investigator badly by the morning. I said meet me in this particular parking lot, which was somewhere out by Studio City, and I'll pay you $20/hr. Now there's a lot of sketchy stuff that goes on out on the Left Coast – Mark could have been hooking up with a serial killer for all he knew, but he went with his gut instincts to trust me and that was his first good hunch.

Like I said, something about Mark stood out from the beginning. His honesty and his willingness to learn were great assets, but there was something else – what I describe as "MOS" or Master of the Streets… There are senses in this world that you can't learn, you can only develop them *if* you have what it takes, and Mark did.

Most of my work those days was what we called *domestic*, the real term for divorce mediation. That role that took us to places where cheaters thought they would never be "made:" seedy hotels and cultural palaces, fancy restaurants and race tracks. Mark mastered the skills of fading into the background while tailing people, dressing and acting in a non-descript fashion while using cameras to capture the moment. (In those days the cameras were much bigger and more difficult to obscure!)

Needless to say, he proved us both right and became my go-to-guy for tough matters. Mark could do it all: gather intelligence, use a disguise, sweet talk someone or dig through their trash if they wouldn't talk. He could take a great telephoto picture and also learned the value of tearing a $100 bill in half to guarantee getting a confidential informant to call you back…something to do with the tail numbers on an airplane hidden in a private hanger.

It didn't matter if the client was a low-class addict convinced their partner was lower class than them or the client was high society. Southern

California offered some "high profile" work, such as the case of the guy who had just been on the cover of Fortune Magazine. Our customer was the wife, who at first thought her husband may be involved with drugs... in the end the scenario involved hidden property, family and friends that knew the truth already and a baby. Some high speed driving and high rent locals later and Mark was cracking the case – all the while keeping just far enough back from the target vehicle during a hunt.

A few years down the road Mark was engaged by the same woman due to the quality of his work together and the fact that he never got caught. Mark had since moved back to New England, to his roots in Brockton MA, but nobody ever filled his shoes in my agency. His energy, his sense of humor, his clarity in the pinch those are the qualities I miss that come back to me when reading the pages that follow. Mark is also a man to respect for the care he has given his children, including two twin sons who suffer from Duchenne Muscular Dystrophy. I hear the next book is about his experience raising money for this cause by entering the ring as a mixed martial arts fighter...

As for the book you hold in your hands, all I can say is: Mark is right. It does happen all the time. Enjoy!

Introduction

It's a cold winter's night and I'm at Logan airport, outside of Boston, awaiting the arrival of my mark. It's hard enough performing any surveillance in an airport, not just because of the heightened security measures, but because of the masses of people who arrive every day at the worst designed airport in history. I've taken care of the fact that you can't sit in a parked car outside the arrival terminal with a well-placed *fifty* in the hands of the State Police. Now my problem is I don't know whether I'm looking for a man or a woman.

It all started with a call from a brother PI from the Midwest who had a client that was in a custody battle with her soon to be ex-husband Dick. Seems like your typical boring domestic right? But we never get the easy cases, it seems – Dick is transgender and is going through a sex change to become Dixie. Our objective on this matter is to find Dick being Dixie so the client can present this to the court. He/she is looking for split custody while my client is looking to remove any and all visitation given the sudden lifestyle change and the effect it will have on the children. She might be acting out of spite –and I'm not an advocate of taking a parent away from the children, but she might have a point… At the very least a little debriefing or some education might be required for the kids. But who am I to judge? I always say that as long as it's a legal and an ethical investigation – and the check clears – it's all good.

So my agent Jay and I are staking out this transportation carnival (he's combing the baggage carousels) for a man *or* a woman with one grainy black-and-white photograph. Jay's getting stressed out, as he often does, and I'm the one who has to calm him down. As my protégé, I've avoided giving him the traditional, how-to-be a private eye training. There's no way to prepare for a situation like this, really. When I first started teaching Private Eye 101 at the college level, I looked back through my textbooks and magazines about how to set up shop. You know, how you should present yourself as a professional investigator: what kind of business cards to create, what your website should look like, how to dress. And then I thought, fuck that. I cut out all of that crap and wrote my own stuff.

Take my website, for example – people complain it's too personal. Other PIs say, Geez…your face is plastered all over the place, even your name is there! You're supposed to act in secret, you're supposed to be a Private Eye. But the public comments on my site all the time: there's stuff about me on there, there's stuff about my family, and they can relate, they can connect. Here they are doling out a couple of grand on a cheating case, they don't want it to be so covert like an 800 number, you know, fill out this form and someone will get back to you in the middle of the night. Get over yourself. It doesn't matter if people see me – the cheaters I'm looking for, what are the odds they're going to see my website?

Same thing with my storefront. When I first started, I put up a big sign: **MWC INVESTIGATIONS**. I thought I was the shit – I thought it was going to be like 7-Eleven, people would just walk-in – knock knock – Hey I need a private eye? Can I get a pack of gum also? But what woman or man is going to walk up to a Private Eye office and say, I think my husband or wife is cheating on me? No, you do it discreetly, over the phone or you meet them at a coffee shop.

I have always gone against the grain of what a stereotypical Private Eye is. I'm not your traditional, ex-FBI, stuffy-ass, looking like a cop Private Eye. When I go out to interview a witness, I wear running shorts. Maybe my Boston Red Sox hat and my "TAPOUT" T-shirt. You see some dude come up to you with a shirt and a tie on, looking like a cop, he's going to get you to talk to him, but he's not going to get you to open up to him. And that's what you're looking to do as a P.I. – you want to show up and be welcoming, make people feel comfortable with you. The fact that most P.I.s are grey and old and have guts, that's not the problem. The problem is they are ex-cops that think like cops. I think like a criminal.

In my opinion, cops make everything too black-and-white. They base everything on reputation, what people have done in the past. That's what they always go after – forget about what actually happened the night a crime was committed. They want to bring somebody's character into question, plant that suspicion in the jury's or the judge's mind that they *could* have done it, not that they *did* do it, necessarily.

That offends me. Let's face it, the defense is already at a disadvantage. The DA's office has the state police, they have the local police, they have power, they have badges and they often do things that are illegal to push a case through…or get information. They threaten people, threaten to take their kids away, report them to DSS, whatever. Now don't get me wrong, 99.99% of witnesses on criminal cases ARE CRIMINALS. They all have records, they have all been in other cases – criminals travel in packs, they hang out, it's part of the deal. If someone gets arrested for shooting a gun, and there are other people around that are witnesses, well, those people also have records, and they may also have guns. But my job is to get relevant intel, not to judge anybody.

Ex-law enforcement officers, on the other hand, seem to have a hard time with that. It seems like a normal transition, crossing over to be a P.I. after you retire from the force…but a lot of them have a hard time when it comes to this work. After spending 20 plus years on the other side, arresting people, they don't know what to do with the fact that EVERYBODY IS GUILTY OF SOMETHING. They come into the game not being able to dismiss it – it's like when you've been cheated on and you reconcile as a couple, but you can never really forgive or forget.

An apt simile, I think. What these newly minted P.I.'s don't realize is that when you don't judge anybody it much easier to find people. Take my snowy night at Logan for example. Eventually I did what any bored individual would do with three and half hours to kill in a airport would do – I came inside and started checking out the rental car specials. (Okay, maybe not everybody puts as many miles on a car as me or needs to have a variety of vehicles to run for disguise). And there at the Hertz counter I found Dick/Dixie. Or should I say s/he found me, checking me out. The eagle landing itself, as we like to say in the P.I. business.

Dick wasn't the prettiest man to ever attempt the cross-over. In fact, he looked a little more like Dog the Bounty Hunter behind the long flowing head of blonde hair. He had that nervous energy of someone on the lam, who is still out for a good time…and that's the way I view cheaters in general. Maybe they did it and maybe they didn't do it. Maybe they had a reason to cheat – most do – maybe it was a good reason, and maybe it wasn't. This work may not take me into the crack alleys as much as my old line (and who doesn't miss a good crack alley every now and then?) I don't go to the prisons as much as I used to. But as I've found out, the human heart too can be a prison: just as dark, just as unfair at times, just as real. These are my stories then about my travels in pursuit of what really goes on in the modern day lives of American marriages. Hop in.

Chapter One: Man's Best Friend

My mom and dad were way ahead of the times in raising me and my sisters to be open-minded children, to never judge or discriminate against anyone. That could be because we were all adopted. My mother couldn't have kids so first they adopted Mary. Then one day Catholic Charities called and said, "We've got Mary's biological sister, Susan, as well – do you want her?" Shit, yeah! That's like hitting the lottery – that never happens! I'll go into my whole story of opening up the case file on my adoption later, but suffice it to say, my parents never held it over our heads that we were adopted or made us feel weird about it. We were shown love and discipline, we struggled against our parents' authority just like any kids would, and we came back together just like any family embrace that happens to make it through in this world.

It's my destiny to spend my time chasing cheaters and suspected cheaters around (I don't want to get ahead of myself here, but suspected cheaters *are* cheaters 90% of the time, we all have that gut instinct and a ton of my business is just telling people what they already know). But I think it's because of how my sisters and I were raised that determines how I do it. I will take any case: transgender, religious cult – that some of other P.I.'s won't touch, like they have some kind of morals. These intolerant people think that love and infidelity only comes in the form of being a heterosexual, but that is not at all true. We are humans and Bruce is going to love Bill and Jane is going to love Judy. What does this mean? Bruce can break Bill's heart and Jane can cheat on Judy. The involvement of P.I.s in alternative relationships has grown in importance since certain states have begun allowing gay marriage – the stakes are that much higher now with the division of marital assets being a factor in a break-up.

Long story short, a case is a case. When I received the call from Stan he was just as heart-broken as anyone who suspects she or he is being cheated on: distraught, angry, confused and in denial. A lot of what you do in my business is coaching and counseling; Stan comes to me with "strange gut feelings" that his live-in man is cheating on him (see my thoughts above on how accurate those feelings turn out to be!) – and we have to go through the entire list of the signs of cheating...

Besides his gut instinct, Stan and his partner, George, were experiencing a lack of sex – in fact all of the elements of their intimacy were changing; George was staying out late, and being evasive about his whereabouts or making up excuses; and finally, George wanted to take a trip from Florida where they lived to Provincetown, Massachusetts, *alone, in order to get away and think.* Provincetown, for those of you who don't know, is on the tip of the Cape and is one of the most expensive waterfront areas on the East Coast. P-Town, as we call it, is filled with great shops, gorgeous natural vistas, and seafood that is out of this world. It also happens to be one of the gay meccas of the world, populated by buff men, butch women, drag queens, and the occasional "normal" nuclear family, strolling the tight cobblestone streets amidst banners of rainbows and very "out" behavior, looking for once like they are the minority!

This is actually relevant to the case, because even though P-Town is a very questionable place for a gay man to go to be alone, a trained investigator must consider all of the options. Perhaps Stan's partner did need to get away, perhaps the issues at home were getting to him and he needed to think – it wouldn't be that unusual for him to want to go somewhere were he felt comfortable, where he would be surrounded by enough other people of his own orientation that he could relax. Stanley seemed appeased by this idea, but informed me nonetheless that he was on a planned business trip to DC and he just could not focus until he knew what was going on with his man. *On the Mark, Inc.* was instructed to go ahead with our surveillance.

Stan also happened to be very paranoid and was terrified that we would be "made." What does this mean? Basically it means that the *suspected partner* finds out that the *suspicious partner* has hired a Private Investigator. This in itself can ruin a relationship – if the suspected partner is innocent, they can feel that hiring me amounts to a fundamental lack of trust, almost akin to cheating itself. Of course if they are guilty, they might still try to swing things back in the direction of blaming the accuser, so to speak. I tried to tell Stan that people who are accused and not guilty most often just get sad, whereas people who are cheating are further "outed" (not in the sense he was used to) by their angry, defensive and self-righteous reactions.

No matter. He wanted a foolproof way to not get caught trying to catch his partner. Hey, that works for me, too. Just recently I got a call from a irate man who said: "I know that my crazy-ass wife has hired you to follow me, assholes, so stay away!" This was funny because all the client and I did was exchange a few emails and wouldn't you know it, she left her computer on? I instructed Stan to delete all emails sent to me, or to set up a separate account in order to communicate with me. I told him, basically, that everything that could be used to catch his partner could be used to catch him: where he made his phone calls from (getting a phone card and contacting me that way can solve this problem), where he drew the money from to pay me, etc.

But the best way to make sure he would not be caught would be to have two agents on the case instead of one. A lot of times clients don't want to pay for this – as Stan didn't initially, although as you will see I was later able to talk him into it – but it makes a huge difference. If you only have one person you have to get closer if you're tailing in a vehicle and you can't be as creative – there is a greater chance that you can could either lose the subject or if you fear a compromise you have to intentionally back off and terminate your efforts. But if you have two cars you can pull switches, go down parallel roads, go off and on –

this also applies to a foot tail, which this turned out to be. Bear in mind that if the person you're following is guilty – even if they've never been followed before, even if they are overly self-confident (read: arrogant) and convinced they are getting away with something – their natural guilt will still function to have their senses more keyed up. Somewhere they will be on their guard, and two agents is a great investment.

But like I'm saying, this didn't start off as a foot tail – this started off as a needle in a haystack. Literally, all I had was an 8x10 photo of a handsome guy and his Bassett Hound. Please. I quickly learned that the whole town is filled with Davey and his dog Goliath. Stan's partner George was already on the Cape, so that meant I couldn't trace his travels – I was setting out for a 39 year old short hair Caucasian athletic built man in a crowd of thousands.

Where to begin? Well being a good P.I. I first started by calling several Bed & Breakfasts to see if I could get lucky and find George registered as a guest there. "Pretext" phone calls, as they are called, are used by everyone from law enforcement, to bill collectors, to P.I.s in order to obtain third party information using some sort of false pretense. There's different laws surrounding what you can and can't do – basically, you can't put up a pretext with government agencies, banks, or phone companies... but a B&B? All that required was a little acting: one of my ex-girlfriends Heather used to give me shit all the time, saying that I used different voices when talking to different clients, especially when it's part of the sell… I think she was worried that she didn't know who I really was, or tat I don't know who I really am.

A lot of times P.I.s can overthink things, brainstorm all these elaborate ways to get information when in all actuality sometimes a straightforward method works best. What's wrong with just calling and acting pleasant? I'm looking for my buddy George with the Bassett Hound, has he checked in yet? No? Okay, thank you. I'm supposed to be meeting him. I'm checking in myself. I'm not quite sure which B&B he's checking into. I'm having a hard time getting a hold of him… Whenever the atmosphere got suspicious on the phone, I would speed my voice up – sometimes if you talk so fast you confuse the hell out of them, then they want to help you out just to get you off the phone. Anything to avoid them getting a manager. If they say let me get a manager, you're screwed. Might as well hang up!

No luck with the B&B pretext search – George could be staying with his shadowy new friend if such a person existed, or he could have checked in under another name (which would have been a definite sign that not everything he was doing was on the up-and-up). There was no choice but to hoof it and search old school. That first day was demoralizing – I was attracting a lot of attention as a single man making eye contact with every other man who had a dog, whether sitting outside at cafes or strolling the densely packed streets. Six hours went by and I was becoming delusional, which happens when you aren't striking it rich –

you start to play games with yourself. You know, maybe that is a Bassett Hound and not an English Bulldog?... I decided I needed some way to be able to see more clearly, to be able to withdraw further into the background so I invited Heather, the now ex-girlfriend, the next day for a nice field trip to P-Town.

I'd been training Heather as an agent for a few years when this case came along. She loved it – she was in school to be a psychologist, so for her, scenarios of *who* is doing *what where* always turned into *why* they are doing it. And I'm not going to lie – there are times when her insights into people's character provided the break in the case I have needed. But Heather's best asset to me was always her personality...well, and her fake tits. She is very outgoing, and people are just drawn to her. Plus, we had a good rapport together, we knew how to flow together – if we were out at a bar, and were trying to talk to someone and get information – the fact that we really were in a relationship made it seem more believable... we're just hanging out at the bar, you know, like costars that act better on the movie set because they really are in love. Plus, I bribed Heather with a little shopping – we decided we would go spend the money we were earning from the case while we were working it, mix a little business with pleasure.

When you're doing this kind of foot tail it doesn't really matter how quickly you move – going in and out of stores, buying a few things for the house and some wedding type bands (hers with diamonds, mine a platinum band) made us just as likely to run into George as actively combing the streets like we were on a manhunt. I often think in a situation like this, the best thing to do is to sit still – and let the natural parade of humanity pass by your feet until…

Bingo! We locate the subject, his dog, and an unknown man walking hand-in-hand down the street, casually window-shopping. The adrenaline rush at this moment is like a drug – after all the down time, all the keeping yourself ready and alert like cops on a 12-hour stakeout then the two guys finally pull up to do the drug deal and you rush out to make the arrest – it's a great feeling.

A great feeling that is until you stop and consider the other side, which is Stan's human emotions. Even though I'm pumped up, excited, feeling like the cat that just brought the fucking dead bird home – you know he is going to be crushed. When you get a client like Stan, a little sad, a little sullen, where you can tell he really likes this guy and they have had a long-term relationship, you have to treat the moment of truth a little gingerly. Sometimes you get the client who's like: I want to catch the mother fucker, I know he's been cheating on me, forever – although those people can shift on you, they act all tough and then once you tell them the news, they switch personalities and fall apart – men are far worse than women in this regard, by the way. The men fall apart a hell of a lot worse than the women do.

At this point, I just phoned Stan and gave him the facts. George and his friend were walking very closely and seemed to be into one another like they were two school kids with a crush. In my eyes George was busted right then and there. Everybody has a different idea of cheating, you know – the President of the United Stated gets a blowjob, and that's cheating. Other people consider it cheating if you confide secrets in someone other than your partner, if you just talk to someone else without being up front about it. For some people you need copulation for it to be cheating.

And then of course there is denial. Stan did not want to face the truth. He instructed us to stay on George until we had more evidence or *self-torture* as I like to call it. Sometimes people say, "I just want to know what s/he looks like" – this happens all the time – "just get a picture of him and her." It's weird, it happens in every case: ego gets involved. The client is hurt – hey, I do it in my day-to-day life; there was a time early in our relationship when Heather and I had broken up for a time and you get obsessed with knowing what that other person looks like – you just need to know. Then I think we take that and use it as therapy, because we're like, Geez, that person's ugly. They don't have what I have. He can have her, she can have him.

Stan was one of us then. He wanted Heather and I to stay close, to continue following George and Mr. X, which we did all day: we watched them share a lobster roll, watched them eat an ice cream cone at sundown, and captured it all on video. This was so much easier with Heather along with me; if I had been by myself I might have attracted their attention – "Hey, who's that creepy guy who's filming us?..." But with Heather's natural way with people, it was easy to play it off. "Hey hon, get over there," I called. "I want to get you in the camera, get underneath that sign." And she flashed her warmth putting them at ease, while I captured her in a tiny corner of the frame while the rest of the scene was consumed by our two lovers and their Bassett Hound eating the crumbs that had fallen beneath the park bench.

I reported back to Stan, explaining about all the video I had of the on-street activity, and it was still not enough. Some people really need to see footage of their partner banging someone else – I'm not even kidding you. I explained that we could not get this unless we snaked a camera under their hotel room door which is illegal. I like making money, and Stan was paying us by the hour, but I said, "Look we've got them holding hands. A.) He lied to you. He said he was going to clear his head. B.) He's with another person. C.) They're sharing a fucking ice cream cone and a lobster roll. Hello? He's cheatin' on you, pal!"

Not enough. What else can I get, Stan wants to know? Well... one time in Chinatown I followed a couple into a shithole apartment on Stuart St., watched them walk inside and gave them 30 minutes to settle down to business, then knocked on the door with a camera in my hand. The person opened the door, I snapped a photo and screwed my ass out of there. It's one of the reasons I stay in shape, because you never know when you're going to have to run like a bat out of hell, but I still got the shot of the individuals completely undressed. That was early in my career – is this really necessary, Stan? Stay with them, he commanded us, stay the night and put it on my bill.

Okay. Twist my arm. Heather and I tailed them back to their B&B (which goddammit was one I had called yesterday and the room was under George's name – I found this out just to satisfy my own satisfaction – and the stupid desk clerk had just gotten it wrong) – then we checked in ourselves and took turns heading to the room to freshen up. We checked that there was only one mode of egress and kept one person in the lobby to make sure our subjects didn't exit. Soon after Heather left for the room George came down to the lobby desk to make a reservation at a local restaurant. I then told the desk clerk that I wasn't trying to be rude but I couldn't help but overhear the recommendation he gave George for a restaurant, and could he make us a reservation at the same place since we were unfamiliar and new to the area? Heather came down, looking hot, and I proceeded up to the room to rig up the hidden button camera.

There was a time when hidden cameras were large and bulky and not at all practical. When I first started my practice I used to rent equipment from a retired State Trooper who ran his business out of his basement. I would show up and it was like a scene out of James Bond where his assistant would show me his latest creation and I would rent it for an assignment. I remember one time I had to go into this bar to record a lady who had a wrist injury, but who was accused of working while on disability. I couldn't bring in my regular camcorder and phone cameras weren't yet invented so I went with these large, ugly ass Buddy Holly glasses that had a pin camera attached to them. Nobody hit on me that night, that's for sure. But I did get my footage of this woman with the *wrist injury*, twirling bottles like she was Tom Cruise in the movie Cocktail…

But now times have changed. Now I have a color digital video recorder the size of a pager that clips inside my suit, with a wire that runs to a button on my shirt. (I have about thirty different colored buttons depending on the type of shirt I'm going to wear). I'm paranoid about not getting footage, so that night I tested it like four or five times… by the time I got downstairs Heather reported that our couple had already left the B&B about ten minutes before us. As it turns out, they were enjoying each other's company so much, and sauntering at such a leisurely pace, we actually passed them on the way to the restaurant. I pondered on these two: they really did look like they were in love. I don't know what life was like for George and Stan or why George needed a fresh start – it's not for me to judge, like my parents always told me. You assume the cheaters are sinners, but life is always more complicated than that.

When Heather and I grabbed a table close by in order to overhear their conversation and video the body language, we didn't hear any conversation like, "Geez, we pulled the wool over Stan's eyes," nothing mean-spirited like that. In a little while our appetizers arrived, and the couple started to hold hands and kiss one another. I finished up my heirloom tomato salad and proceeded to the men's room to inform Stan that the job was over – George was cheating on him, I had the video, and the report would follow upon my return. I told Stan he didn't owe us any more money. Sometimes you just have to put an end to the self-torture. Or maybe it was because I wanted to get out of there and go get laid myself? Stan said thanks but no thanks, he didn't want the video, and that he was a fool for not trusting his gut. Then he kindly thanked me for my efforts. I'm glad I don't judge, because I would have had no idea who was right. Case closed. Time to stop thinking and enjoy our night on the Cape.

Chapter Two: Even the Score

I'm supposed to be the cheating expert, right? Which means, what, exactly? Well, one thing it means is that when an old girlfriend cheated on me once, I busted her in a heartbeat. I knew all the signs we've been talking about, I knew what her next move was going to be, and I knew how to connect the dots in a discreet way. I was like, seriously, did you think you were going to get away with it? Now it also stands to reason that if P.I.s are experts in cheating, it would make it easier for us to pull off the act. But does that we would – just because we can? I'm sure some P.I.s do cheat just like some cops are dirty or some firefighters are pyros, but like anything in life, it's a case by case basis. A great chef can create a wonderful dish and then recreate it at home, but…that's a bad example. We're looking at an entirely different situation here.

Some of my girlfriends leading up to (but not including!) my wife, Stephanie, were always very concerned about this – if I was in the can or I'd just fallen asleep and couldn't get their phone call, then I'm cheating. I'm cheating because I catch people doing this for a job. I would say, "I investigate homicides, too, and drug felonies, but you don't see me gunning down the neighbors or swallowing kilo bags of cocaine and getting on an airplane for Key West?" That would puts their mind at ease a little. In truth, I didn't blame them for their worries; you have to be a strong-minded person to understand the life of a P.I. Even if you don't start out that way, believe it or not, if you are around one enough you eventually morph into one.

One of the reasons I didn't blame any ex is because of course the temptation has been there. Women clients come to me lonely and confused, probably just like men and women are vulnerable in front of their therapists, priests, doctors, and so on. If they suspect their partner has been cheating they might be out to get revenge or at least explore their own attractiveness. It's like I was saying before, everyone wants to know if they still got it: when a case is nearing its end, they want to see the pictures of their partner's new lover to satisfy their curiosity; when a case is just getting going, they send me pictures of themselves and try to get me to express interest in them.

One of these women was Melinda, who was from out west, some part of New Mexico. She got in touch with me because her husband was a businessman and was taking a lot of work trips to Boston. Some new and all-consuming project that he wouldn't talk very much about – Melinda was convinced that this project he was so engrossed in was actually another woman. Living in a big city like Boston we have a great deal of businessmen and woman in town for conventions and business meetings. Not in and of itself a crime, of course. But traveling on business without one's husband and wife you can often feel lonely and try things that you may not do at home. Crawl out of your skin and be a different person, let those demons that we all have come out in an environment in which you think you won't get caught...unless myself or one of my brother or sister P.I.s are hired on. If that's the case, you're probably going down.

Melinda sends me a picture of her husband to get started, so I can get a positive I.D. on him. Melinda's in the picture, and I'll get in trouble for saying this, but, yeah, she was hot. Blonde, fit, with either a large set of natural breasts or some very well done fake ones. Hey, I'm still a man! She's kind of going out of her way to send me recon (reconnaissance) material that has her in it, you know, sending me to her website where there's a few pictures of her husband and children but mostly it's pictures of her. I felt bad for her – she had a very bubbly personality, she seemed like a nice person – and here her self-esteem has been reduced to the point where she's calling me at all hours (another thing ex-girlfriends HATE), asking me: why was he doing this to her, look at me, he doesn't look that good any more and I'm looking good, I work out all the time, I run marathons...

Eventually, of course this anxious questioning gets turned on me: why wasn't I doing more with her case, why I couldn't nail the bastard in his hotel room with another woman. That was the only thing she cared about – she was obsessed with getting proof of her husband banging another chick on video.

Okay. All right. But first we have to find his car, Melinda... Melinda as it turned out was ready with this information. Every trip he made she found out where he was staying, what kind of rental car he was driving, what state it was registered in – *even the plate number*. This was definitely one of those vindictive types of suspicious partners, and one who was actually pretty good at detective work herself.

That makes a huge difference. I'm doing this other case right now for a woman in Denmark – her husband flies into the Boston area, to do work at an office in Cambridge, and I don't have shit. I mean, literally, all I have is a grainy, black-and-white picture that came over the fax. It's tough enough to follow a businessman, and almost impossible if we can't track one of his patterns of behavior. I told this woman, "Look, I'm going to have to charge you by the hour, and there's going to have be two of us, and we'll just sit there for two days (outside the office building) and watch every single person that comes out of the fucking place." Because it's hard when you're sitting there and you're watching for ten hours – people are starting to look like him. A couple of times you follow somebody because you're starting to second guess yourself – *could that really be so-and-so?*– no that's not him...then you go back to the building but you don't know if he just left, or what? It can drive you insane.

This guy from Denmark is working in a building that has ten stories and there's 200 people coming out every half hour – the odds aren't that good. But the woman is desperate so we're giving it a try. Melinda on the other hand has all the intel for me – when I go to the suburban office where her husband's working, I find his car right away. I sit there reading the *Boston Herald*, until he shows up. When he gets in his car, I don't need someone else to help me with a mobile tail because even if I lose him, I know where he'll end up (which by the way is a corporate hotel, not one of those hotels where people normally go to cheat, you know across from the strip shows and next to the porn superstore).

So following this guy isn't very difficult; it also isn't very interesting. Every night on the way home he stops at Boston Chicken. No hookers, no woman, no nothing. He goes up to his room – and I don't know what he does up there, maybe order a movie off of Skinimax? That's not a crime, right? I guess there are people that that falls into their definition of cheating… but not mine. Anyway, Melinda's getting more and more angry – "I told you that he was cheating," she's telling me, "Why can't you find out? I want him busted!"

She's another one of those clients who wants me to snake a camera under the door. Everybody thinks I've got this *Mission Impossible* camera that slides under the door and then rights itself while seeking the warmest things in the room to film in black-and-white. I'm sorry, but I'm not crawling through the heating ducts either, that's illegal,that's breaking and entering…or something, that's trespassing, malicious destruction of property if you're taking screws off and removing a heating grate – I'm not Tom Cruise!

"Well, what can you do?" she wants to know. "What good are you?"

Well, let's see, uh, we can "invite" him into the act of cheating. There's a fine line between *baiting* someone into doing something of their own freewill, and *entrapping* them. There's a whole legal discussion here, but basically *entrapping* is inducing an individual to commit a crime that they have no intention to commit. You can entrap someone by threatening them, or bullying them, or continuing to coerce them after they have expressed a desire not to go ahead with the crime.

Baiting someone is totally different. Baiting is just putting something tasty in their path and waiting to see if they'll pick it up. I'll give you an example: I'm doing a case for a girl in Maine. It's a custody matter, her boyfriend's kids were taken away from him, and the mother (this girl's rival) is a crack whore – according to the new girlfriend. So, okay, I send my #1 agent up there undercover to try to get her to engage in some drug activity. Now bear in mind, we're not going to engage in actual drugs, like that movie *Rush*, that's illegal. Jay's job is just to set her up.

We locate the woman at a bar, and Jay goes in. He waits for his perfect opportunity, when he sees her go outside to smoke, then he joins her (Jay hates smoking, I tell him that's part of the job, my brother) and engages her in conversation. They go inside and he offers to buy her a drink, to a table they go, they're talking, next cigarette break and they're back outside – and then Jay starts talking drugs. He's saying, I do this, I do that, do you want to go do something, and she's looking at him like he's got three heads. She actually says something like, "I thought you were a nice guy. I got so much stress in my life and I got to listen to a creep like you?" Jay calls me telling me he almost feels bad... I tell him that'll pass when he gets his check. No, but in all seriousness, I call the girlfriend, our client, back and I tell her – I think you got it wrong. Maybe you all need to find a way to work it out and get along; this woman seems clean and earnest. She's tell me to fuck off and go mind my own fucking business, I tell her you *made* your business my business, she hangs up on me, I run her credit card... that's the way it goes sometimes.

So that's the difference between baiting and entrapping. We're going to bait Melinda's husband. I say we, because I've brought along two associates: a dark skinned, intense looking girl named Kendra with a medium build, and a long, tall blonde named Adriana. I ran over what this guy was attracted to with Melinda, but she couldn't really tell me: short, fat, tall, skinny, big breasts, little breasts, white, black, blue eyes... nothing. So I'm hedging my bets here. No type like President Clinton has a type and Monica Lewinsky with her big trashy bob is going to fit it perfectly, none of that. We're just going to go with two beautiful women, and see if he's going to give into the temptation to cheat.

Plan A goes awry when I attract the attention of the security guard milling about the lobby of the hotel. Security guards, as we all know, are wanna-be cops, not bad guys and gals necessarily, but this one was none too friendly. He makes eye contact with me one too many times, and now I'm being watched. Now Mr. Rent-a-Cop has a hair across his ass for me. Lobby surveillance over, we switch to Plan B.

The Boston Red Sox are playing that night in a big game and the hotel is advertising a complimentary spread of incredible food for their guests. I pull aside a 20-something year-old desk clerk and offer him a little cash tip for his help. I give him half of a 100 bill and say if he can get my mark, his hotel guest, down to the lounge for this playoff game that I would give him the other half of the bill. Perfect idea in theory and if it didn't work, well nothing some scotch tape couldn't fix!

You think people are going to get offended? You think they're going to get moralistic, or concerned for their job and report you? You think people are even going to be curious and ask questions? You would be surprised. People are just motivated by the money. Not trying to be cynical, I've just learned over the years how easily a small investment opens doors. Luckily, this kid was great and performed his task better than some of the investigators I have used over the years. I listen to him as he gets in the subject's head, talking about the food, and how he should experience Sox Mania while he's here from a part of the country where they don't even have baseball, and freakin' twenty minutes later our guy comes down to the lounge. Awesome.

Kendra and Adriana are already in the lounge waiting for the game to start, while I'm at a nearby cocktail table eating some chips and drinking a beer. Not that this guy was going to notice, but you can't be sitting there drinking water – if someone for one minute starts thinking you're not there for the reason you should be there, you're on the road to ruin. So Kendra and Adriana are sipping cosmopolitans (made Red Sox red by the addition of too much cranberry juice, I'm told) – just sipping them because their judgment can't be impaired. That's another reason I'm there, to make sure everything remains safe and copasetic.

Not that I really have to worry about them – they're trained to know when to stop, which is going to go to come in handy in this case. Normally we wouldn't go anywhere near this guy's hotel room; we would get him to proposition one of them (or both) and then leave. Of course, as we know by now though, everyone has a different definition of cheating. For Melinda, flirting isn't going to be enough. But I'm still not going to allow a female and a guy to go behind the closed door of a hotel room together. I don't know this guy from Adam (his name is Andy, for the record). Everything Melinda is telling me about Andy being mild-mannered, besides being a cheater, could be bullshit – this guy could turn into a totally different person behind closed doors. He could come on to one of my agents, they could get scared, he could get violent...so we decide it's going to be: *get him off the lobby floor*. We get that settled before we even walk into "The Auld Mug," or whatever the hell the lounge is called. Once we're airborne in an elevator, or on his floor, I'm going to be right there, and the gig is going to be up.

The first pitch is being thrown out and not long after Andy walks in, strides over to the two girls and pulls up a bar stool. With any luck we'll have this over by the third inning, I'm thinking, as these girls are giving off some major sexy body language along with some subtle touches and lots of laughter. It's working like a charm; Andy's buying them another round. I'm in the corner fiddling around with some of my covert video equipment. You can video people without their consent but you can't audiotape them in Massachusetts. The video does capture some audio, which might render the whole tape not permissible in court but half of the shit we get isn't permissible. What happens most of the time is the evidence is hinted at – the subject is threatened with it – to the point that they cave in, and give the wife the house, just to avoid having their name trashed to their kids or in the community.

Based on my observations, the subject seemed to be more into the blonde (Adriana). He was paying a little bit more attention to her, his eyes wandering over her long frame. The girls were doing great. The only problem was that the game was a real nail-biter with everything on the line. Everybody out our way talks Red Sox, so the whole crowd was into it: the bartender, the patrons, my server – this lounge is the place to be and for the moment nobody's going anywhere.

I order an appetizer. By the time I finish it, it's the bottom of the fifth. There are worse places to be – I'm kind of hanging out with my friends – kind of, not really. I'm trying to keep calm; the moment you get too anxious and try to *make* something happen is when you blow the whole thing. You got to let things play themselves out… but by the seventh I've had it. The Sox have built a lead and I text Kendra to meet me near the bathroom so I can try to figure this one out.

She tells me what I think I've been seeing: that he's relaxed, and having fun with them. Only every time they try to turn up the heat, he mentions his wife! His wife and his two beautiful sons, how he is in town on business more often than he would like, but he misses them all and can't wait to get back to them.

Say what? This dude was too perfect for us to be watching him. Kendra goes back to the bar, and I go outside to my car and call Melinda, saying, "What is up?" I've been watching Andy – from Mayberry – for days now and gotten nowhere; now I have two hot chicks on him and all he can talk about is his wife and kids and how happy they make him.

"I cheated on him," Melinda blurts out.

"What," I say. What the fuck did you say?"

She says, "I've been having an affair for a long time… I feel guilty… I was hoping that he would be doing the same thing, or at least be tempted to, so we could even the score and get our marriage over with. I want the kids but I don't want to go to counseling or anything. I just want out…"

I'm not stunned very often, man. But I was just like, "That's pathetic. This job is over, and I'm billing you for everything" (hinting of course that if she didn't pay me, I'd always have the option of turning over the details of this case to her husband).

Then I go back inside. By now, the Sox are up 7-1 and on their way to turning this ALCS against the Indians around. I pull up a chair on the other side of Andy and ask if I can join them? I buy everybody a drink and we all watch the end of the game together, trying to be as normal as we can be in a fucked-up situation created by some fucked-up woman pulling the strings.

Chapter Three: TV Tease

People want to say that I'm a publicity whore, but what they don't realize is, there's a method to my madness. In this internet world, it's basically all about exposure; there's a new way for people to research, for people to find you, a new way for you to be "discovered." And I'm all about being discovered, because I've got bills to pay. My website has increased my business exponentially, and I mean exponentially the way they taught you in school. My business hasn't "multiplied" or "really added up," it's gone up exponentially: 1 client, 2 clients, 4 clients, 16, 32, 64...

There are a lot of reasons for this, and one of them is I have a look. Christ, I sound like Jordache here. Anybody remember Jordache? If there was a P.I. calendar – you know like they have those firefighter calendars, I'd be a candidate...and that's not because I'm some stud or anything. It's just that I'm fit, I'm relatively young, and let's just say that most of the Private Eyes I've run into over the years aren't the most beautiful people in the world.

I've gotten a lot of hits, a lot of calls from people over the years who like my look. They like the fact that I put my face out there. In addition to those clients of course, I've met a lot of people scouring the internet: scumbags, attorneys, soldiers looking for work when they return from the war, female college students trying to break into the business who send me pictures of themselves in lingerie, people looking through the *Pink Pages* who see my advertisement: "On the Mark Investigations: Best Dick in Town! We are here to SERVICE you...."

Some of my correspondents over the years have been Hollywood people, scouring the internet, looking for P.I.s. Hollywood has always had a fascination with Private Investigators, and I've always had a fascination with Hollywood. As a kid growing up, I sat in my room dreaming of being on TV, singing into a hairbrush, you know the routine. My next door neighbor had a theater growing up – which I thought was kind of weird, until I realized that theater *is all girls*. That's when me and two other friends got involved; we decided to do drama because all the hot chicks were doing it.

Since then, I've had my phases, including a brief stint as an actor and model in California. In 2006 I got a call from a company called Half Yard Productions, who was looking to do a TV pilot for TLC. They liked the fact that I was from the Northeast, they liked the look I had on my website...yeah the only problem was they really liked my website. My site gives the illusion that I have this big, thriving firm, with like ten employees: investigators and legal consultants and forensic consultants. It's all smoke and mirrors, of course, and that goes for the whole business – I don't have a problem exposing that. Apart from a few P.I. firms that mostly do a lot of insurance work, we're all mostly mom & pop organizations out here. Everybody else that I work with is a consultant, a vendor, and I'm creating the illusion of a team. An illusion – just like anything else in "real" life.

Except now the TV company comes and they're saying, "This is great! We're going to get everybody in your organization involved." So I had to kind of shuffle a little bit, and think: Who do I got? I got Jay. Jay, that's about it! The production company also wanted a female, so I chose Susie Friday. Kind of funny, right? Like Joe Friday from Dragnet – that was her real name, and you can't even improve on that. Susie was cast as the attractive blonde who works with the so-called "dream team." She was the friend of a friend, and she wanted to be involved in the business – so that was the way we crafted her character. It wasn't necessarily a lie: she'd been working with me off and on for many years now; I'd call her on specific cases – and she'd been bugging me for years to work full-time. So that's how we spun it to the producers. .

So that was the team. In the opening scene of the pilot, Jay, Susie, and I are striding down the street like the opening of the movie Armageddon, heading towards the camera with this big voice-over and heavy-toned music like America's Most Wanted. Because, let me tell you, TV and real life don't mesh too well. Here are these Hollywood guys who think they're going to hop in a van and film every case I'm working on. I tried to explain to them that it doesn't work that way. First of all, there are privacy laws and wire-tapping laws, we can't just hide TV execs in vans to pick up audio on cases, especially criminal cases. You want to be part of getting some guilty-as-well jerk off scot-free? And second of all, these are my clients – you can't just freak them out with model releases and destruction of their confidentiality. If you want to pay me up front, we can do that! But if all this work is going to be on spec, then you're just going to have to chill.

We were going to have to make a case up. We were going to have to act it out, didn't they know something about that? We would act, and they would do it up with their fancy editing to make it look realistic. There was this one particular scene that we wanted to do: It wasn't really based on a specific case, more like on a thousand cases I've worked, but I could see it in my mind's eye: following a cheating spouse and using covert equipment to bust them.

First we had to find the cheater. I said, I know! Victor was the producer for my former *On the Mark* radio show; I chose Victor for a couple of reasons. First of all, he's a seedy-looking Italian dude with a mean streak. Secondly, he's always expressed an interest in my business – although everybody does that. Do you think in other lines of work people come up to you and say, "You know, I could do what you do." I get so many fucking resumes – everybody thinks they can act stealthily like that's all there is to it. Everybody can act because nobody knows who they are! I get so many of these emails, I can't answer them all. Like I mentioned above, I do answer the ones from soldiers, the ones that say when I come back from the way I want to do bodyguard work, do P.I. work, would you give me advice?

Bu the third reason I went to Victor, was I trusted him. And that's what I told him – yeah, you're interested in what I do, you fit a look, but most of all, I really need people I can trust. I told him I also needed a woman I could trust that he would be pretending to cheat with. That was when he said, why don't I just use my wife – besides the fact that she's my wife, we've got instant chemistry. I said, perfect. Her name was Robin – I'd never met her before at the time.

I told them both what they were going to do: Victor, when you're ready to leave work, you're going to call Robin, just like you were really cheating. Say, "Hon, I'm leaving the studio, I'm going to meet you at the mall which is only about 2 minutes up the street." Then when you come out of the radio station you're going to leave in your car and you're going to drive to the mall. Robin, you're going to be there waiting in your car; when Victor pulls up into the parking lot, you're going to hop into his car and head to the bar...

A lot of the allure of the show, and I hope it does get picked up, wasn't necessarily the cases, as much as it was the interaction between the characters, the dialogue and the back-talk. That we didn't make up. While we're tailing Victor, on a made-up case, Jay and I are still arguing about who's better at the mobile tail, me or him. Jay hangs way back, so far that he loses people sometimes. I get the call, and I know what it's going to be from his tone of voice: You fucking lost him didn't you? Me, I can get a little aggressive – although I've only been made (detected by the mark) twice in 12 years. Jay's telling me we're getting too close to Victor, and convinces Susie we're going to get made (even though the cameras are rolling!) Dude, I'm like, "He's so focused on going to get laid, he's not worried about us."

The couple hugs, they embrace, they kiss, and we get it all on video. Victor looks like he's really having fun. Robin hops into his car and we actually do lose him for a little while on the road. "What'd he do, put that thing into Hyundai rocket blast?" Jay asks. We catch up to the couple at a bar, the Rivera Café. It's this place in Bridgewater that my friend owns; it was good PR for his restaurant and he was more than happy to let us shoot it there. We let all the people there know, the regular patrons, that they were going to be extras – I take up a seat at the far end of the bar, but before I send Susie down to where Victor and Robin are, I give her a little coaching:

"Look Susie," I tell her like she is the true ingénue, "this is your great opportunity. I want you to pull it off. This is your great acting role, so I want you to ad lib, improvise…" I told her I wanted her to go in, and strike up a conversation with the couple. You know, who are you with, how long have you been together, see how she introduces herself, stuff to give back to the client.

Meanwhile, I'm going to be sitting on the other side of the bar, videotaping them with my hidden camera. It worked perfectly! While Susie was talking to them and I was videotaping, there was chemistry, there was body language, there was a little hugging – would have been enough for almost any client. I say, almost because there are those people who you tell: Alright. Your husband was out with this girl, our female agent approached him and your husband told her that he's not married and he's been dating this girl for a year. What else do you have, these kinds of client want to know. Well, besides the fact that he's not where he says he's supposed to be, that he's meeting this girl at a bar, that they're kissing when they meet, and they're introducing themselves as together and not married…what else did you want? This is when I apply my "pain-in-the-ass" tax: You want me to keep following them after that, your rates just went up 50%.

In this "case" though, after we captured the couple on video, and I called my client to tell her what we had, she said: "That's enough, break off the case."

I think of that often, of me sitting in that bar watching Victor, and Robin – who I thought was a lot more attractive than what Victor would have had for a wife. No offense, dude! You know what I mean. Meeting her was very surreal, because I had known Victor for a while but he didn't like bring her into my life. So I didn't really know her, which is what I told myself, when it came out that Robin had been cheating on Victor for years, and had been cheating on him *while we were filming that scene.*

When Victor found out, he started blaming himself: I'm just not one of those people who's in touch with my sensitive side, I work too much and I'm not catering to her needs. Okay, maybe, man – but that's not a reason for her to go out and cheat? How about a little conversation about it first?

Victor started getting obsessed with the fact of her cheating; it was fucking bizarre to watch. Hollywood, come to life! And it wasn't good either – because Victor, I'm telling you he had the ability to snap and be violent. I've seen it, I saw him do it during my radio show, and although I think he's a good guy, he's got that little something missing.

Who was she cheating with? Now I got to help him – and this shit wasn't getting mocked up, either. Why do you want to know, dude? I got to know. Okay…she was cheating with a guy who owns a used car lot where Victor bought his Hyundai. You can't tell me that makes you feel any better! She was cheating not only at the time we made our pilot, but for a while before that (all it takes is one person to slip…)

The problem is, this kind of search has no end. Victor wanted more; he started to pull documents and receipts. He broke back into the house they owned together, okay – not good! This always goes against my advice. You have to hire a professional, and not just because I'm trying to make money. It's because you might get into a situation in which you can't control yourself. He's borrowing his friend's car and tailing the two of them, what's he going to do, confront the guy and beat the sit out of him? He's asking me: What should I do? Should I go talk to the guy?

Leave it the fuck alone! Leave it fucking be. It's not his fault. God knows what she's been feeding him. She could have been feeding him shit for as long as they've been together – that you're an abuser, that she doesn't love you, that you're not together any more, how does this guy know. Granted he sold you a Hyundai or something, but…how's the car running? No, seriously; stop the self-torture. You want to boil down my message for people who have been cheated on, that's it: Stop the self-torture.

Chapter Four: The Jehovah's Divorce

I was raised by a devout Irish Catholic father, and a devout Italian Catholic mother. They tried their best, but church didn't do much for me; growing up we used to have to go to Mass every week where the Bible was spoon-fed to us – even then I didn't see how you could believe in something you couldn't see. The only break in this tedium came from my father's brother, a 40-year veteran of the Priesthood. He was "well-connected" for a priest and ran a large, local church. That guy could give a sermon: funny, edgy, manipulative and imaginative. They were set in the here and now as opposed to some other imaginary time and place.

Maybe I'm just not a faithful person, but as I got older I came to believe that some of these devout believers have got to be hiding shit. I know people are raised and conditioned in a certain way, so that might explain some of it. And I know certain people find religion for other reasons, such as to ease the pain, or to distract them from their problems, even to inspire them to do good and prevent them from doing bad. But I'll bet that if you surveyed the more cult-like religions, like the Jehovah's Witnesses or the Church of Scientology, you would find some of these people come from very checkered pasts. Born agains and ex-criminals, right-wing religious leaders and diddlers – they're all extremists, there's no grey area. You're either a crackhead, or you have to jump over to be reborn, there's no middle ground.

This prejudice of mine started to change when I did some work for the Church of Scientology. I met one of their investigators in court and we were making small talk. She asked me if I was interested in doing any research work for the Church, that was about ten years ago. I was just beginning to figure out how not to let any of my personal opinions get between me and an organization with unlimited resources! Part of being a Scientologist is similar to being a Christian: you have to give them a percentage of your salary. There are different levels of believers and you have to pay to make it to the next level.

It's funny the way financial need can encourage you to look at your stereotypes. I went to a meeting with three of the powers-that-be, in a gorgeous brownstone in the Back Bay section of Boston. They seemed normal. They had conducted an investigation on me previous to us our getting together, and had a file on me – which was fine, I had nothing to hide.

The one thing that was pretty wacked, was the *e-meter* test that they put me through. This thing looked like one of those Rube Goldberg contraptions, you know where household objects are strung together in a very complicated way to accomplish a simple task? The *e-meter* is supposed to be a device which measures electrical resistance and can be used in the auditing process to determine truths and non-truths – I just saw what looked like toilet paper rolls, a bunch of string and a cardboard box.

They told before the interview ended that they just wanted to do one more thing, if I wasn't opposed to it. They put some kind of lotion on my hands – hey, I figured if you're not injecting me with anything or making me take medicine, I'm in! I had to hold on to these cylinders while they asked me all kinds of questions. "Was I a double agent?" "Was I a spy?" "Who sent me?" "What were my true intentions?" I loved that question! "Uh, to make money?"

Looking back on it, maybe it was a psychological test as much as anything. First of all, would I consent to do this, then did I object to any of their lines of questioning. Maybe they were watching what my eyes were doing, or my expressions. It didn't freak me out, but I did start to feel bad for them. This level of paranoia could only be built up by a lot of people being out to get them. They do have a horrible reputation in the media, but in my experience they were *nothing* but *real, nice* people. In the decade that I worked for them, they never tried to pressure me to join their cult or group or whatever. They've also done a lot of good things, too – one of them is a Hollywood actor who made a contribution to my charity. Some my other associates have shown up at my events, the ones I've hosted for my boys. They've cared about me and about my family, which is more than some of my so-called "friends" have done – you know who you are!

Maybe the Church of Scientology just needs some good P.R., instead of this aliens abducted Katie Holmes' brain crap. We don't really make an effort to understand the beliefs of these people. Like remember the Jehovah's Witnesses when we were kids? Even my devout father and my devout mother, teaching us the Golden Rule: Do unto others... would be like: "Shut the damn door in their face! Don't answer it!"

I think it's something about them coming to the door that freaks people out. This was in the '70s, when you could go door-to-door. I still see them out there, and I want to tell them, "Look. I've seen shit in this town, okay? You go knocking on every stranger's door and eventually you're going to get abducted and kept in the basement as a sex slave. I'm sorry! You're going to get to that house that says, "Sure! Come on in..."

Maybe the Jehovahs just need a uniform change. You know, like a sports team that's had a bad logo for years? Do something different, like come to the house dressed in Hawaiian shorts, as opposed to their plain suits and skirts Or maybe it's just like anything in life – you have to meet one person to understand that they're really more like you than you could have imagined.

My turn came when *On The Mark* got a call from female Jehovah's Witness, who suspected her husband was cheating on her. We met at a Dunkin Donuts, my favorite stomping grounds, to go over the details of her situation. It was a particularly hot summer day, and this woman was overdressed. She looked like she was one of the Amish, for Chrissakes! She was young, too, an attractive and very sweet woman who was just so embarrassed to be doing what she was doing. She was hurt by her situation...most people are. The divorce rate among Jehovah's is very low and I was soon to find out why – because they make you jump through fucking hoops in order to get a divorce!

She needed two agents, doing surveillance together. We had to get video footage of two unmarried people entering a house before sundown and not leaving until sunrise. Then we had each had to sign an affidavit and agree to testify if summoned. All this, just so she could convince the Grand Poobah or whomever at her Kingdom Hall to let her get a divorce. It was too bad shouldn't just call up a local probate and get a lawyer. Everybody else just drafts up the papers to be served, but okay! Maybe we have a niche here, Jay!

After the first night of surveillance, this wife told me what we had obtained didn't meet her criteria, it had to be for two nights *in a row*. If it wasn't, we would have to go back to square one. In case this is the first chapter you've picked up, my criteria is: What is more money? I'm sorry life and my responsibilities have crafted my philosophy. Besides, it *has* made me more tolerant. Who am I to fucking judge? Maybe it should be a whole week – that would be a great idea! It's not cheating if it's not a solid week of shacking up together, minimum, and we have to stick around for two weeks just to be sure? That would be fucking fabulous.

At the time I didn't do any research, I just took the woman's word for it. I never knew for sure if that is what Jehovah's Witnesses had to do. Maybe some of it was for her? She did seem set and determined when she came to us. She had *heavy* intel, I'm talking dates and time, make and model of the car, the address and where to see it from best. This trench-coat wearing schoolmarm had been doing some work!

The location in question was a Boston brownstone, an upper scale "Back Bay" residence similar to the building where I had met with the Scientologists. Whatever the connection was between cults and the do-re-mi, it was working for me. I also just love working in the city. In the city people are moving too fast to care who you are. It's not some rural area, where any time there's a car rolling down the street it's a big deal. It's easy to video tape and to see people coming and going, which can often be a problem. Plus, Jay and I both have a city, in-town kind of look to us. We could be the pizza delivery man, and you wouldn't even notice, you'd be too busy looking at your pizza.

Really the only headaches in the city are the meter maids. I don't know how many of them are named, Rita, but I can tell you that not many of them lovely. Many of them are old bureaucratic bitches that have been overworked and overtired for the last thirty years collecting that paycheck. In this particular part of town it was a residential area, it's all permit parking, and all the spots were are taken. We basically had to set the surveillance van up in front of a fire hydrant.

P.I.s in Massachuetts have a license, that looks like a driver's license, but this one woman was just too crabby. She's bitching at me, and it's at that point that Jay moves in.

He's feeling her, you know, making her laugh. He's explaining to her that we're bringing down somebody who has more money than either of them could ever dream about. You can see the appeal of that start to spread across her eyes like a smile. In fact, we didn't really know much about the guy we were tailing, but it did the trick and she let us stay where we parked the whole time she was on duty!

All we really knew about the dude was that he was "spiraling out of control," which just basically meant he wasn't practicing his Jehovah's beliefs. He had already left the church – but that wasn't enough to sanction a divorce. And neither was the fact that this dude and his new lady had spent last night together from 4:00 PM to 7:00 AM, behind closed doors. They had to do it again!

At 4:10p, just like clock work, the subject rolls up with his paramour (who looks like a dude) and video is obtained. The first night, Jay and I actually had to roll back the footage because he swore it was a dude. "No, it wasn't, you're fucking blind!" "Dude, it was. This explains everything…" When we viewed it for like the fourth time I was able to convince him; he started picking up on some feminine vibe or aspect to the woman's gait while they strolled inside.

P.I. work can also be excruciatingly boring, by the way, have I told you that? The sun goes down; lights come on inside the house. They're inside living their life, making dinner, watching TV, while your life is basically just waiting for them. On our second night of surveillance, the summer heat had just broken, but the windows to the Brownstone were still open and we were able to get some additional footage directly into a dining room area. As much as you think it's going to be him doing her on the dining room, it's really way more of him crossing the room to get a book, or crossing and re-crossing and re-crossing the room because he can't figure out where his glasses are.

Besides, all we needed was documentation that they didn't leave until the morning. It wasn't like we had to catch them in any act. In fact, our client specifically told us she didn't want us to go to the door, which is HILARIOUS when you think about it. What, it's okay for you to interrupt me when I'm eating dinner to tell me I'm going to Hell, but I can't bust your husband when he's breaking a religious commandment and civic law? I think it would have been priceless: two scruffy-ass looking private investigators knocking on the door, with the proper pamphlet shit in our hand: "We're Jehovah's Witnesses! We'd like to talk to you about your faith…" Can we just have a minute of your time?

Nope, no action for us. No real-life porno going on across the street. Nothing but two dudes inside a van, one taking a nap with his shoes off, and the other focusing endlessly on the front door of a house. I think this is how mine and

Jay's friendship really took root – all those hours of surveillance. You know those people who even though you don't agree with and they get on your nerves, you still have a connection with them? After fifteen minutes of silence someone just says something and it flows easily into another whole field of discussion?

"I should start advertising, Jehovah's Divorce, as our specialty. Put my OTM pamphlets on their cars at every Kingdom Hall within a 50 mile radius of my office?"

"You're stupid if you think BC has a good basketball team. Or is a good school for that matter."

"This new girl is definitely not as attractive as the old girl, but I don't know what she's doing behind closed doors. Maybe she sucks a good cock, I don't know. I don't know what women read in those Cosmopolitan magazines, but let's cut to the chase: suck cock."

"Maybe she's saying the right things."

"Maybe she gives him anal."

"I'm not going tell the client that."

"Why not? Give her the heads-up."

"I don't have to tell the client anything, remember? We just have to get footage of them both leaving in the morning. Video obtained, file closed."

"Right…"

"I'm thirsty."

"Did I ever tell you about my father's brother?"

"The dude who ran the shrine?"

"Yeah…Do you remember when all that scandal was breaking about the Catholic priests? I was so glad that nothing was ever tied to him."

"Sure, it would take you down with it."

"No, it wasn't just because of the media frenzy, it was because that was a guy I believed in."

"Right?"

"You don't believe me?!?"

"Take it easy…"

"Anyway, I was worried, just because all these stories were coming out – abo everybody – but then I remembered how we used to rent a cottage on the beach near the shore every year. I remember one year, my father's brother was with us, and we were in a local convenience store. This is when the girlie magazines were out in circulation, they weren't wrapped in plastic behind the counter. For some reason I remember myself walking around the corner – I might have been like 8 or 9 years old – and there was my uncle skimming through a Playboy."

"SHUT up."

"I don't know – maybe it was a Sports Illustrated swimsuit issue. All I know is that when I remembered it, I said, I can trust this man."

Interlude: How to Cheat

Cheating is wrong, plain and simple. In this chapter I am going to give you some practical advice – if you are going to cheat – about how to increase the odds of getting away with it. Does that mean I condone it? No, but a lot of people have asked me for my advice on this subject since I catch people cheating for a living. And besides, I'm not so naïve as to think that every marriage or partnership is solid and deserves to last. What would a good analogy be? It's wrong to go 95 miles an hour down the road, but if you wear your seatbelt and you don't talk on the phone, if you plant your feet and use your radar detector, well, then, you might just get away with it. You could potentially be fucking with everybody's life, including your own. But this is not a moral chapter, this is a practical chapter. So on we go: My top ten rules for getting away with cheating.

1. **Never bring your lover to your home.** Nobody abides by this rule, by the way. This only applies if you're living with the person you're cheating on of course, and it *especially* applies if you're a man. Women are born detectives: they'll find a strand of hair, they'll catch a whiff of old perfume. Women are worse than you parents when you had a party, remember, back in high school? Something is bound to go wrong – it's Murphy's Law. Your new lover goes to

clean herself up and you're not covering her every step, there could be something that gets left behind. At the very least, bang someone with the same hair color as your partner!

In all seriousness, you might get your partner's schedule wrong. Or something changes, and they just show up...happens all the time. And then it's like the blues song:

One way out, baby, and Lord I just can't go out the door
'Cause there's a man down there/Might be your man I don't know

Why would people bring their lover to their house anyway, because they're cheap and don't want to pay for a hotel? Maybe they're just extremely cocky. Or it could be spite, like a cat spraying their pee around. If you won't give me what you want then I'm going to take care of it on your side of the bed! I think it also depends on how kinky you are. Some girls or guys get off on screwing in the same bed for power – but ASSUMING you don't fall into any of these categories – then go to a hotel.

Hotel, motel, B&B, it doesn't matter – just remember to pay cash. Don't ever put anything on a credit card. If you pay with a credit card, the next thing you know you stick the receipt in your pocket, then you forget and your wife does the laundry, "What's this?.." You don't need to be intimidated or embarrassed – people pay cash all the time. Besides, you're not going to the Ritz, anyway, most likely, you're going to the Red Roof Inn – these people know that you're coming into bang. I know, I've talked to them, trying to get information out of them. Hey, come to think of it: We're in tough economic times…maybe some of these hotels should advertise? You know, "Infidelity welcome, $49.95…"

2. Never call your new companion from a known phone number. In the old days people used to call from a pay phone instead of the home phone, but obviously there aren't too many of those dinosaurs around anymore. Then the cell phone entered the mainstream, and for a while that was safe. Now, even if you delete the number there are still SIM cards that can pull off all of the information of who you've dialed, and the bills themselves probably come to some central place – like the house. You might go over your allotment for texts, your partner might get the phone company to release your records (who you called and for how long), pretending that they don't understand why their bill is so high?... Don't put it past your spouse to do some pretext calling of their own!

Your best bet is probably a company cell phone or to make your calls from the office. If you are going to use your personal cell phone, you have to limit your talk. I'm not even going to get into Tiger Woods talk, but let me just say that everyone is guilty of breaking these rules from the top of the societal ladder to the bottom. Set the boundaries, set the rules. You may think that the days when one lover calls the other in the middle night – and then hangs up on the second ring are over, but you'd be surprised. A lot of my clients get tipped off by just such amateurish moves like this one.

The only exception to this rule is if the lover is a friend of the family – I'm not passing judgment here…it happens all the time. Where else are you going to meet somebody? Then it may be weirder if they don't call the house – once in a while. You just have to play it by ear.

By the way, all ten rules boil down to the same rule in the end: be safe and be smart.

3. Don't use the family computer. It's too risky. Even partners only somewhat versed in the computer will be able to access the cookies in your browser, if they are motivated. You may think, "Well, I'm not looking up escort services, I'm fine!..." You're wrong. You're looking up cheap, *local* hotels online – and you aren't planning a vacation with the family any time soon…you're done. Don't send emails from your home computer either – the chances are too great that you will leave your email account open. Do all your dirty work from the office.

Porn on the home computer is a different story – I think that's a matter of interpretation as to whether that's cheating or not. Every guy looks at porn. I think if a woman hacks into a computer and sees porn – except kiddie porn, of course – she should be happy. That should solidify that the marriage is tight, because if the husband's looking at porn, they obviously don't have the guts to go out and cheat. They just need a little extra flavor and they're doing it via the internet. It's like a woman sticking a dildo in her pussy when her husband's on a business trip, and thinking about Brad Pitt – there's no difference, men are just more visual. Are these facts? Or is that my opinion? My opinion based on fact? Or based on observation? I leave that to you to decide.

4. Keep a low profile. Don't make a reservation at the local restaurant. In fact, don't go out at all, or if you do go out – if you feel like you owe your lover "a date," then make it as far away as you can comfortably drive and get back in the time span you have allotted. Remember, Murphy's Law? It's not just that somebody's contact lens case next to your bed at home, it's running into a family you know at the Perkins Diner! The truth of it is, you really can never go out and expect not to be made. If it's just – what do the kids say these days? – "A friend with benefits" – then it should just be strictly sex. You meet at a certain place and you have sex. And you leave.

The problem is people start to get attached to each other and then they start to fall in love. It depends on how cool the other person is. I think it takes a special person – I don't want to be too sexist, I'm just relating what I've seen – I think it takes a special woman to strictly just want to have sex and that's it, and not fall for the person. It might start that way, or both people might say that's what they want, but one person changes their mind. It helps to have parameters ahead of time, and keeping a low profile is one of them. But if one person wants more and they're not getting more, then it becomes Fatal Attraction all over again: "I will not be ignored!" That's one of the big risks that you take, one lover exposing the relationship and contacting the other's spouse – and a lot of times the lover will use that as an ultimatum. "I want you to leave your husband or wife for me, or else." Which brings me to my next rule...

5. Get leverage. There's no way to know ahead of time if someone's going to get psychotic, so get some leverage right at the beginning. It may sound evil, or at least devilish, but think of it as a kind of outlaw pre-nuptial agreement. It could be something they're doing at work, something that they've stolen, or some misdeed they've committed, get the details and get some proof. People are surprisingly open when they're first getting into a relationship and that's the time to snag some piece of information that you might need later on.

The best kind of person to choose to have an affair with of course is someone that you can reasonably expect you won't need ammunition on later. Maybe it's someone you have had the opportunity to observe for a while, someone that you work with – over the years you have come to understand their lifestyle and their personality, and there's only a mild chance that they are going to snap on you. The worst kind of person to choose is someone who's not in a relationship. Not only are the odds greater that they are going to get more attached to you, but someone in a committed relationship has more to lose with kids and a husband or wife at home.

Getting leverage can involve hiring a P.I. – Hey, there's a good idea! – to do a background check on them. Now, they aren't going to have great character if they're cheating but it might help you find out if they generally have their wits about them. Take photographs, record their admissions, and don't feel guilty: you haven't done anything with the information yet. Besides, all's fair in love and war...

6. If it's just sex you want, don't even start a relationship. Why take the risk? Escort services and prostitutes are 1,000% better. If paying for sex throws you off, consider hooking up on a business trip for a one night stand. Use the old tried-and-true method: you meet someone at a bar, give them a fake name, you have sex. And that's the end of it, you're never going to see them again. A lot of conventions have turned into a kind of fantasy land for these kinds of activities. Your new lover's life is at home; your life is at home. There are no traces left – what happens in Minneapolis, or Key Biscayune, or wherever, stays there.

By the way, just so you don't think I'm being sexist, more and more women are doing this now. They're complacent and miserable at home, their husband's got a big, fat gut and doesn't pay any attention to them – so they travel and they hook up. I'm just saying…

7. Don't get too confident. I suppose this goes for anything in life – when you start to get too confident in your abilities, that's when you start to slip up. Like I said earlier: be safe and be smart? Well now I'm adding: be scared.

Too confident means that at this point you've been getting away with cheating for a little while, and then you start breaking my rules. You bring your lover to your house. The phone rings at some weird hour. You use your home computer. Whereas before you were very strict with the process and with covering your tracks, now as life has gone along you start to get sloppy. Everybody gets lazy after a while…and then it's too late when you get caught.

8. Don't tell more than one BFF of your affair. Now, I know what you're thinking – why would I tell anyone? Well, you shouldn't, but most women will tell their best girlfriend. Most guys will probably only tell another guy they're close with if they need an alibi – more on that in a little bit. People who run their mouths about their affair are just asking for trouble. You might not think so – you're at Spin class, talking to some girl and you're telling her about the guy you're dating…except she happens to know someone who knows your husband, and it's going to come up in the weirdest ways. Why even take the chance? To show off? Everybody knows somebody and some people know a lot of people.

As far as guys go, I think most guys adhere to the *guy code*: an unwritten rule that we have amongst our species. Just as most girls have one trustworthy friend, so most guys have the guy who will cover for him. One of my local buddies was screwing around on his wife for a while – and he used to use me as an alibi. He'd call me up and say, "Hey, Mark, the next time you run into my wife, we had dinner last Tuesday night at such-and-such restaurant…Okay? All right? Thanks, man!" This particular woman liked me, too, you know, the father of kids … but as her husband's illicit relationship went along, it got more and more involved, and she started not liking me anymore. She thought he was out having too much fun with me, while I was sitting home watching Family Guy. Whatever. Guy Code.

9. Use Protection. You don't want to bring any diseases home to your spouse, or your new relationship will be exposed in a heartbeat. Protection – in case you didn't know – also protects against impregnating someone? Just thought I'd mention that that would also be bad.

I know I've mentioned this in a previous but don't change your sex patterns at home either. Don't start asking for more just because you feel guilty.

Don't shy away from having sex just because you're "in love" now with somebody else. And above all, don't try out your new funky, kinky sex move on your partner without being fully prepared to explain where you got THAT idea from...

10. Deny, deny, deny. Do you remember that song from a few years ago, "It Wasn't Me?" 'She caught me on the counter... it wasn't me. Saw me banging on the sofa...it wasn't me.' If they haven't caught you red-handed: it wasn't me. It wasn't fucking me.

Say the worst thing you can imagine happens, your partner comes home and there's a feminine product in the toilet...and your partner's not menstruating. It's not what you think it is. It's just not what you think it is. My sister was here, she had to use the bathroom – what can I tell you? Then you get on the phone as fast as you possibly can, "Listen, Sis. You got to cover my ass this one time. Remember when we were kids, and you came home shitfaced? And I covered for you that night with Mom and Dad? All right, you were on the rag and there's a tampon in the toilet, in case my wife calls. I'll explain it to you later. Blood's thicker than water. Bye!"

Chapter Five: The Friend

What is cheating? What constitutes cheating is an on-going debate that will never be settled, because it is all *relative*. The dictionary says cheating is the act of being "sexually unfaithful," yet for one of my clients his wife is cheating because she had a cup of coffee with another man and my client didn't know about it. Of course the fact that his wife lied about it made it even worse – this is where cheating is really much more about trust than it is about a pair of people getting their rocks off.

But even suppose we are talking about sex – what kind of sex? How much? For how long? I know what you're thinking – you're thinking you know exactly what cheating is. And you do – but only for you! When the President of the United States told us all last decade, "I did not have sexual relations with that woman" – was he lying? (And how many men have used that excuse since to "just" get a blowjob?) A friend of mine refused to have sex outside her relationship, but when an old flame called her up she masturbated with him on the phone. Is that cheating? Is it cheating if the old boyfriend knows? Or is it cheating only if the new boyfriend knows?

What about porn stars who go home to their marriages – "What'd you do today at work, honey?" Or, "Who'd you do today at work, honey?" It's an agreement. And since it's an agreement, rather than a fact (like concrete is stronger than a skull is a fact, or I'm not going to remarry my ex-wife is a fact), agreements can *change*. There's this scenario which comes up often – in fact it happened just yesterday (as I am writing this) with a potential client.

Someone calls me, and as I'm talking to them, you know starting to feel them out, get a vibe as to why they want to hire me, *what they may be worth financially*, I realize quickly that they're not telling me something. They have beyond the normal level of embarrassment, and that's when I find out that they're having an affair. Mary wants me to check out her boyfriend, Tom, but Mary and Tom are already married – to other people! Mary wants want to know that he's not having more than one affair! She's suspicious and actually angry: Damnit, she deserves to know that he's not going out on her!..that he's not going out on his wife with anyone but her. Wacky, man.

That's what happened in this case I had last month. My client was a Boston policeman; he was married, but he had met a girl in a kiosk at the mall. He really liked her but before he left his wife he wanted to make sure that this new girl wasn't cheating on him, by giving happy endings at the massage parlor. I guess she had two jobs – I don't know what she did at the mall, maybe she worked at the *Piercing Pagoda* or at *Shia-pets*? What a great place to meet someone, really. She might have been one of those bitches that rubbed lotion on his hands. Ooooohh, I love the way you massage my hands, let me leave my wife for you. Apparently this woman also worked as a masseuse on the side, and the cop wanted to make sure she was on the up-and-up at her other place of employment.

What was funny about this case was that I never actually met the guy who hired me – it was his friend who called, and his friend who met me. At first, I really tried to put the screws down. I looked my contact right in the eye and said: "Look. Are you sure this isn't you? I don't give a fuck, okay? You want me to tell you some stories so you know I'm not judging you?" Here, read my book – that's what I should have said, although that would have freaked him out, I'm sure! But no, this really was his friend; at one point he actually called the cop while I was sitting here, and was talking to him on the phone. All right, whatever. It's not you. Even if it is.

Now you may be wondering, why doesn't this policeman just use his connections? He could run a background check or an employment history more easily than anyone else. First of all, cops are pussies. You show me a cop who walks around like a big man, full of bravado and machismo, like he is above the law – and I'll show you a cop crying into his beer to me about the fact that his wife is cheating on him. I get more cops hiring me to follow their wives or girlfriends than any other single profession. Actually, you know what? I take that back. Cops aren't pussies, they're human. Things happen to them. Things happen to their kids. It's inevitable.

It's probably good that the cops don't take matters into their own hands, just like I warned my friend Victor against doing in Chapter Three. There's no sense getting into a murderous rage when a little third-party objectivity might yield much cleaner results. Plus, these days everything is flagged in their computer systems: every time someone orders a criminal check or runs some plates, there's a record of it. These cops can't jeopardize their jobs.

And finally there's the embarrassment of the whole thing – if they start snooping around they're sure it's going to get out that their wives are cheating on them because they aren't laying them good. I don't know whether you have to have a well-developed sense of paranoia to join the force, or if it just comes with the territory of wondering every day who has a gun and who doesn't, but the policemen I know have been the most paranoid people on the planet. This guy, and his friend, were channeling that paranoia hardcore; they never gave me the actual client's name, they wanted the job done YESTERDAY, and they micro-managed the whole process to the point where it couldn't help but get fucked up.

Originally, they found *On The Mark, Investigative Services* through a television news story featuring my business. Every Valentine's Day it seems we're interviewed for a segment about cheating. Cheaters have to spend Valentine's Day with their significant other, but then they'll try to hook up with their lover either before or after – that whole week is usually gangbusters for us. Restaurants love it, they're bursting at the seams (don't forget those guys who are still married to their mother and have to take them out too!), and P.I.'s love Valentine's Day as well. So maybe this regional exposure would have put my clients at ease that we knew what we were doing?

Maybe not! The Friend met me at Dunkin' Donuts and starts telling me what OUR plan is. He has the masseuse's personal cell phone number, and he wants us to call her and make an appointment for TONIGHT. I'm trying to argue with him: she's going to wonder where we got the number from, why can't we just do this the right way? Let me call the massage parlor, find an open appointment with "Ginger" for two or three days from now?..

No, the Friend's telling me, it has to be tonight. There's always more to it when someone gets us involved. But sometimes there's more to what there's more to what there's more to, you know what I mean? At first I though it was the client's police ego that was getting in the way, and that was why he didn't think it made sense to listen to the experts – why he couldn't conceive that there might be something about setting up pretext calls in the right fashion that he didn't know about. Cops don't need pretext! They need a warrant (sometimes) and a gun and boom! They're in.

But then I realized – the cop didn't *want* to catch her. He was looking for something else: justification. Some part of his brain or someone else that he had confided in had said, you have to check this new girl out. So now he can say that he did, and still hear what he wanted to hear in order to move forward and leave his wife. He didn't want the truth, which he could have given him if we had moved forward the right way and nailed her. No, he wanted us to botch the job – that would be the deodorant on the stinky armpit that was going to give him the justification to leave his fat wife at home who's not giving him head.

I remember arguing for my approach to this case twice. That's usually my limit; if the client says no after that – all right, you're the consumer! It's like that fast food joint: *Have It Your Way!* Jay and I are the fucking Burger King of Private investigators! It's amazing what $1,000 cash in an envelope will do, if you're not being asked to do anything illegal. Too many P.I.s have too much pride when it comes to "professionalism." *"If I don't think things are being done the right way,"* they say, *"I won't take the case."* Please. I got four kids. These P.I.'s are probably retired cops, collecting a fucking pension.

Like I say, if I'm not doing something illegal, I'm really fine with it. And I might even be fine with it if we are doing something illegal, which it sounded like we might be from the "plan" that was given to us. The cop wanted to make sure that his new crush wasn't giving happy endings. So the question was: How do we find that out? Someone was to schedule an appointment with her, and then at the end, in addition to $100 for the hour, you lay down an extra $300 in cash…and wait and see what happens. That was the protocol according to the cop and his friends in Vice.

Well right off the bat, Jay's concerned. "That's definitely going to be cheating according to my wife!" he's telling me. Well, what if we break off after the masseuse moves towards giving Jay head or the "happy happy joy joy" handjob? That's not good enough, according to the Friend, who goes on to assure us that the one thing the client has done is make sure that there will be no sting operation anywhere in effect tonight.

So it's really just a moral question. I'm in a relationship, Jay's in a relationship, we have to find someone to go get a blowjob for free. Shouldn't be that hard, right? I call up Ted, a rook in the truest sense of the word, some kid right out of college who's always bugging me to get into the business, and he thinks I'm kidding.

"Fuck you, Mark."

"No, seriously."

"You're going to pay me $200 to go get a fucking hummer?"

"Maybe, I said, maybe something will happen."

"And nobody's going to bust me?"

"Absolutely no chance."

"You're fucking kidding, right?"

I tell Ted that if he doesn't shut up and get down to my office in twenty minutes, I'm through with him for good. Eight minutes later he's pounding at the door. We calm him down, give him some water and rehearse him before he makes the phone call – we want him to make the call because it to be the same voice that Ginger hears all the way through.

And he's really good! She's suspicious (of course), but he's talking about his back, and the fact that his chiropractor's on vacation; he's describing in great detail who gave him her number – such great detail that she's probably too embarrassed to admit that she doesn't know who he's talking about – and she agrees to see him that night.

On the way to Chinatown this kid is about as happy as I've ever seen anyone. It's like that line when Sean Penn was interviewed for the Actor's Studio, and the question came, what do you expect to hear in heaven? "You've been a good boy – the eight ball (of coke) and the two hookers are in here…" Ted's in the backseat going over the description of Ginger, the photographs, a dozen times each until we let him out of the car.

He enters the massage parlor, and gets led to Ginger's room. There's soft music playing, there's a scent machine somewhere; Ted's face down on the table when a woman enters. She starts massaging his back trying to find the problem area that he's identified. It sounds just like the woman he talked to earlier today, but when she tells him to turn over – it's not Ginger. There's no way that it's

Ginger; forget about hair color, the height is wrong, the nose is different. Ted doesn't know what to do.

After the massage is over, Ted comes out holding the $300 like it's infected with some kind of spore.

"You didn't lay it down?"

"I didn't… The girl…it wasn't her!"

Sure, Ted's green. But it was the cop and his Friend that fucked this whole thing up from the beginning, because they didn't really want to know the truth. They didn't trust us to do our jobs and were just using us as pawns in their dysfunctional game.

"You laid it down," I told him. "And she took it and you didn't get anything for it."

"But I—"

"You laid it down."

And this time he gets it, sliding the money into his jeans.

And he doesn't just get a handjob, or even a blowjob – he gets a full hour in the sack with this chick who, shall we say, is not a virgin. Ted says he got extra because she liked him. I don't know about that. I do know that he wasn't cheating on anyone, so you can't call it that. I think you might as well call it love.

Chapter Six: Follow the Leader

By the time someone calls me to follow a spouse that they suspect of cheating, 9 times out of 10, they are. My clients usually go through three different stages beginning with: suspicion. Something sets them off; something's not right. Especially if they aren't the particularly jealous type, there has to be some kind of trigger. Then, they enter stage two: detection. They start doing work on their own, following up on signs, checking up on their spouse, until they go from *warm* to *hot*. Then they get to the third stage, the most unfortunate one of them all: denial. Just when they get close their mind starts playing tricks on them and the most obvious indications to you and I – textbook displays of infidelity – they just won't want to accept it.

Let's look at these three stages in a little more detail. Suspicion can arise in just about anyone, and if we're honest with ourselves, we've probably all experienced a little paranoia in our lives. Now I've had some clients who are truly disturbed, who have seen no signs of cheating whatsoever and who still had me follow their spouse around for years. That gets into the grey area of control: my client wanted to know who his wife was spending her time with, where she was spending her money, where she was spending his money... It really was a pathology.

In the next chapter I'll tell you about the case of the woman who never cheated but who I still was paid to follow to all four corners of the U.S.A. But let's say you do notice something concrete. It doesn't have to be – and it usually isn't – walking in on your spouse banging someone in your bed. The clues can appear almost insignificant except that your inner voice is telling you they matter. Your spouse is working late again. They're evasive about where they are, or where they've been and then get overly defensive when they are questioned, those are some of the classic signs. "You're crazy!" they'll tell you. And you'll want to believe them, but then other little things will happen: they're more interested in sex (possibly out of guilt, and subconsciously trying to make it up to you) or they're less interested, there's some kind of change in their usual pattern. They're going to the gym more frequently, or their grooming habits change. They have a more upbeat attitude because they're in love and, sad to say, it's not with you.

To give you an example of a small, but telling clue, this woman called and told me, "My husband has never worn boxers in his life. It's always been briefs. His family used to get him novelty briefs for Christmas. We all used to joke about how tight those briefs could actually get and his blood still be able to circulate... Now he's got a drawer full of boxers. We haven't been having much sex at all, but I still do the laundry. His briefs are totally gone."

Did the fact that her husband switch from briefs to boxers mean for certain that he was cheating? No, and neither would it mean he was unfaithful if he switched his favorite color from blue to green. The boxers were just a sign that stirred up her intuition – *the fact that she already knew subconsciously that he was cheating* – and helped her turn the corner from suspicion to detection. Once that switch is flipped, it's not about the boxers, it's about the credit card receipt from his favorite restaurant. Except where those slips used to read $80, now they read $190, possibly indicating that he's not going there with his buddies and paying for himself, but he's going there with a date and throwing in a nice bottle of wine. Now it's about the mileage on his car when he says he's just going to work which is 20 miles round trip, but the odometer has an extra 180 miles on it when he gets home.

In the case of this particular spouse, she was willing to do just about anything to nail her husband. I've found that clients exist along a continuum of what they're willing to do on their own before fear or embarrassment starts to set in. Some partners won't even check the cookies on the computer! I'm talking about the most basic investigation: recent web pages that might reveal if someone has been browsing hotels in their local area, for example. Something – anything – that is out of the normal pattern of the way everyday life is supposed to be. These spouses are concerned that they're going to get caught, even when I explain that that's not possible with the technology available on their home computer. But they still want me to check their browser cache; they want me to read the emails, listen to voice mail messages, monitor their phone activity, etc.

Of course, I want the work – don't get me wrong! But I need help, too. You have to be able to communicate with me and give me as much assistance and could help me on the case. A certain amount of intel coming from the client is crucial, and I love the clients who tend more naturally towards detection. The "boxers widow," whom I'll call Carrie, was all fired up after years of what she saw as getting the run-around from her husband, whom I'll call Roy. I know there's three sides to every story, and that Roy had his reasons – however twisted they might be – for cheating, if in fact that's what he was doing. But I confess that I really enjoyed working with Carrie. Everything I suggested she do, she executed to a "t."

She bought a GPS from PIMall.com and stuck it on Roy's car, so we were able to track his movements remotely on-line. That's legal, because the car was registered in both of their names. What wasn't legal was her sticking an extended tape recorder under her husband's driver seat, because in Massachusetts it's illegal to record someone without their knowledge and consent. It did happen to be an excellent way, however, for her to pick up his one-way phone conversations: "Okay, baby, I love you – I'll see you a little while..."

Carrie's blood was starting to boil with the new information that she was uncovering. There's really only so much one person can take. I should mention here that stage three: denial, does not always follow detection. Sometimes a partner or spouse will just flip their lid, and suspicion will go through detection into furious acts of retribution, "crimes of passion" they're called in a court of law. They don't usually carry the maximum penalty for whatever offense (like assault) might eventually result, but they're not pretty – and they're not necessary.

I knew Carrie was starting to get "carrie-d away" when she asked for pointers on how to undertake her own mobile tail. A lot of times when I spoke with her she was over at her girlfriend's house getting her head together – should she use her friend's car? Roy's suspected girlfriend lived a few states away – in New England our states aren't that big, but a car with plates two or three states north could still draw attention. Should she rent a car? I just saw not good things developing. Her mindset was too excited, inevitably confusion and fear were going to get in the way of her objectivity.

"Carrie, what are you going to do when you catch him?" I asked her. "Are you going to hop out of the car, and say I fucking got you!"

"I just want to see the look on his face," she said between sobs. She was a strong woman, but the whole experience was breaking her down. She had been a great detective, but now the question arose: How far did she want to take it?

"Listen, up until know you've been paying me as a consultant. I think you've got to let me and Jay get in there and finish the job."

"Why? You don't think I'm doing a good enough job? What haven't I done?"

"No, Carrie, it's not that – you've been awesome. Rock solid. But at some point, you just have to leave it up to the professionals. I'm not going into the butcher and cutting your fucking meat for you!"

"I'll cut his fucking meat – right off!..." She laughed, and then I knew she was going to listen to reason.

In truth it probably wasn't necessary to go any further than Carrie had already gone. Anything she needed to know to move on with her life she knew by now. Her marriage was over: her husband was lying to her about where he was, what he was doing, and who he was doing it with. No further information that we turned up would aid her divorce in a no-fault state like Massachusetts which has legislated the equitable division of marital assets. If her husband was prominent in their community she might have been able to use video footage to gain a better settlement behind closed doors, or if they had kids his wrongdoings could be entered in a suit to help determine the ratio of child custody. But Roy sold shirts for a living, and they were childless. She wanted to keep on his tail solely because she tasted blood.

We had gotten pretty close by now, and Carrie listened to my advice. I took advantage of this relationship to make a pact with her. I would furnish her with irrefutable evidence that her husband was cheating both so she could get her own head straight, and so that she could throw it in his face (but not literally!) on the way out. In exchange, she would let Jay and I do the rest of the job without any interference.

Our opportunity came when Roy booked a "business trip," and told Carrie only that he was going to Denver. Regarding the specific nature of the business, he was evasive – as he had been for months leading up to this point – and honestly believed that all he had to do was tell her to stop meddling and she would. Then he had the nerve to ask her for a ride to the airport!

Carrie played along, but secretly she was enjoying every minute of it. She delivered to us not only his flight number and his destination (dude was flying from Boston's Logan airport to Providence, about an hour's drive!), but what he was wearing, a recent picture of him, an exact description of the bag that he had checked, and even the suspected girlfriend's name and address. At that point if we had screwed it up, it would have been us who were pathetic...and we almost did. But more on that later.

Jay and I took a ride down to TF Green airport in Providence. Providence is super easy logistically, there's only one way in and one way out, so much better than Logan or God forbid JFK. We had decided to use two agents (and honestly, not so I could charge more... honestly!) and one car. The two agents were so one of us could idle outside on the lookout for the girlfriend's car, while the other one could go inside and greet Mr. Confident at the baggage claim. The only difference is I wasn't going to be holding up a little white sign with his name on it for him. The Providence cops can be real sticklers – did I just say, sticklers? – real assholes when you try wait at the curb. They charge you like $80 if you wait over 90 seconds. But I had a few names to drop and when that didn't seem to be turning the whole trick I went into some details of the case. That convinced them and besides, cops are human. They wanted to see what was going to happen next.

So I'm staked out at the baggage claim waiting for Roy who looks a lot like Vince McMahon. He's clean cut and older, a fit-looking guy with a very distinctive nose. People tend to blend in, so I'm memorizing his face... but of course I've also got a description of the big, black garment bag he's checked and I know that he's travelling with golf clubs. I'm sure that these clubs are a ploy, a this-is-where-I-am-when-I-don't-answer-my-phone kind of thing.

In the meantime I get a text from Jay that he's got a positive ID on the girlfriend. The cops are playing along and letting her hang out at the curb also, because they see that she's the one we've been waiting for. To this point this is about the easiest case I've ever worked on. Roy comes out and greets his girlfriend, Judith, who is average-looking at best. Beauty is in the eye of the beholder, but it wasn't just a line when I told Carrie, "She's got nothing on you!" Because she truly didn't, she had this frosted 80's hairdo and wrinkled power suit, still wearing her sneakers like she'd come from the gym or something. It was all very twenty years ago, down to the large white SUV they both climbed into. And then the kiss.

The kiss lasted about eleven seconds on video. There's the peck on the cheek kiss. There's the kiss on the lips which is still short, and which can still be social either from a particularly gregarious type or very close male and female friends. Then there was this kiss, on the lips with heads moving... like I said before, if all Carrie needed was evidence for herself to move on, she's got it. Your husband's giving another woman tongue and he is NOT in Denver.

But Jay and I knew we were after more, so we pulled out on the highway after the SUV headed... god knows where! These two sure don't! They were getting off the highway, on the highway, stopping at Wendy's, stopping at the gas station, where are they going? I mean, they're here for a tryst, right? Why all the complications?

In the meantime, Jay and I are starting to argue. He's driving, but I think he's staying too far back on them; we almost lost them a couple of times – can you imagine if after all the intel we've got, they get away! Jay's telling me we're too close, we're going to get made; I'm saying these jokers are too focused on stroking each other and getting lost – they have no clue what's around them. Meanwhile we're pulling every stunt in the world: heading down side streets, backing out of driveway to the squeal of tires, breaking every Private Eye rule known to man, and all just so we can be back on the same damn highway heading in the same damn direction we were before.

This went on, in real time, for an hour. And all along they've got a GPS right on the fucking dashboard! It was like an episode out of National Lampoon's European Vacation, you know the scene, where Chevy Chase is driving around the rotary: "There's Big Ben!" over and over again. As it turns out, the one piece of information that Carrie didn't provide us with was that these two actually did work together. We end up at this local breakfast place somewhere in the sticks in Rhode Island and watch as Roy and Judith greet two businessmen in the parking lot. It turns out, they work for some kind of clothing line and these guys are prospective buyers. Now I'm thinking, maybe they aren't lovers after all?... Just like that suspicious spouse who goes from detection to denial, my mind is starting to play tricks on me.

Jay stayed outside in case anybody made a sudden move, while I went into the diner to have some scrambled egg whites and hash browns at the counter. I tried to relax and figure out what was going on. I had just tailed these people for miles upon miles – gotten off at about twenty exits, banging U-turns – it was like *The Dukes of Hazzard*…and now they work together. If Jay thought I was too aggressive before, he should have seen me approach the four of them and ask them if I could borrow the paper that was at the booth next to theirs. I got a good look in both Roy and Judith's face… nope, nobody's paper!

I was feeling the need to make something happen, partly to justify why Carrie couldn't have done the rest of this without me, and partly because I was starting to doubt my own sanity. The business meeting is strictly professional, but he said he was going to Denver – maybe that kiss wasn't as long as I remembered?...

Then Roy's phone rang. He let it keep ringing, although I could see out of the corner of my eye that he was agitated. Finally he got up to answer it and walked right in front of me, yelling at the person on the other end: "Quit calling me when I'm in a meeting! I told you not to bother me. I don't bother you when you do whatever you do during the day..." What a prick. I wanted to slap him for talking to someone else that way, and I didn't even know who it was at the time. But I suspected.

I paid my bill and stepped outside to call Carrie. She was crying but trying to pretend that she wasn't.

"Did you just call your husband?" I asked.

"I know, I know, you told me not to. But I'm just nervous, I don't know what's going on... I'm sorry, I didn't mean to interfere. I won't—"

I cut her off. "Don't worry about it. We're going to bust this asshole."

Two hours later the meeting ended, and they're back in Frosty's SUV. We're in our car except this time I'm driving. Jay's pouting, which I can't stand, so I pick a fight:

"Dude, talk about not being aggressive. Last week I called you and you weren't even at the stakeout, you were at Dunkin' Donuts or something."

"Nuh-uh, I had to take a piss!"

"You don't got a bottle?"

"Ewwww. I'm not like you, you dirty mother fucker!"

"Look you're not exactly the clean cut professional type…"

"Look! They're turning on the GPS! YEAH!!!!!"

And Jay and I started to crack up. We always get over our disagreements quick.

We followed the SUV into downtown Providence, to the Italian section known as Federal Hill. It was August, and it was warm. Their car stopped outside of a hotel in this quaint looking square: fountain, cafes, old men feeding pigeons – it's probably one of the most romantic spots in the world. Jay hopped out ahead and got into the building's lobby just ahead of them, turning on a buttonhole video camera. He was at the front desk inquiring about their availability and rates, while Roy and Judith came to check in to their ONE room. Roy was playing it up too, introducing Judith to the clerk as his wife (Yeah, but that ring was given to her by another guy, dude. She's married – but not to you!) Jay got a room on the same floor and was able to maneuver video of them entering their room, and even picked up a little audio of them horsing around just inside.

I went back to the car and called Carrie. Sometimes I feel like a funeral director, delivering the real time news of the dissolution of someone's marriage. But Carrie sounded different this time.

"Thank you, Mark," she said in a voice that was somehow stronger voice, like she'd turned a corner. "I think I'm all set."

"You don't want us to stay any longer?" Involuntarily, I thought about the fact that her retainer wasn't used up yet, and at *On The Mark*, we don't give refunds.

"Nope. Thank you. I'm good." The line was silent for a little while.

"I'm going to be just fine."

Chapter Seven: Professional Stalker

My style has always been that if a client is willing to pay, I'll take them. That's what makes them a client, right? And if they happen to be a nutcase, well it's the nutcases that make this business go round and round. P.I.s aren't the only business that makes their money off the sick – if you think about it, psychologists, psychiatrists, doctors, lawyers, judges, social workers, orthodontists, physical therapists...everybody needs people who are lost or incomplete in some way. They operate from the same philosophy I've been espousing this entire book – if you're going to pay your bills on time, you're okay with me. Historically speaking, I haven't formed a negative opinion of you just because what you were asking me to do...maybe doesn't need to be done? If someone's a paranoid schizophrenic, and they think the Feds have a wiretap on them – I'm an expert in only one thing – and it's not paranoid schizophrenia!

So that's the backdrop for this case, which turns out to be where even I draw the line. It started out around the time of the Boston Marathon, mid- to late-April. The client, whose name was not Andrew, but that's close enough, calls me and asks me to follow his wife. She's going to be in town for a software convention – she goes away a lot to conferences, seminars, etc. – and he's suspicious that she's getting something on the side. He wants us to check it out.

Fine. The other key piece of information is that she's a marathon runner, and these techie get-togethers always include a local marathon that she and a small group of her female co-workers run for fun.

I had to educate Andrew right off the bat. He started out saying that he wants me to tail her *during* the marathon. Okay, I don't know if you've seen a major marathon being run but you can't exactly drive your car alongside the runners at 8 MPH. And I'm not in good enough shape to run it along with her – throw in the fact that you've got to *qualify* for Boston with a sub 4-hour performance at another major marathon... No, dude. Besides, did he really think she was going to be cheating during the actual marathon itself? Was he that jealous? Between the starting gun out in Hopkinton and being wrapped in an aluminum cape wearing a medal on Boylston Street I think she's pretty safe. I would even wager that she's not cheating on him that night either – unless she's in that good shape!

I convinced Andrew we needed two agents at the marathon, because Boston can be downright hectic that time of year. Jay and I followed her pretty closely from the time she got into town. She attended poster sessions and the keynote speech at her conference, ate her pre-race pasta dinner, slept, ran, went out to dinner again with her friends and flew home. Nope, nothing to see here I reported, thinking of course that that would be the end of it.

About three months later I get a call that he wants me to go to Seattle. It's a bigger convention this time, a veritable who's who of the computer world. It's the biggest thing in her industry, but she's playing it down and that's convinced him that she's making plans to meet someone. I'm a little bit irritated by a trip so far away from home and from my four kids so I name a price that's pretty high. He doesn't blink an eye. He's got all this intel for me, minute details of her day-to day activities – except he leaves out the fact that in Seattle at the end of November is like 20 degrees, with a minus 40 degree wind chill! I've got to go watch this lady run a stupid race, and then she and her friends are going to the aquarium. I ask him: What are you afraid of Andrew, the tiger sharks?

Our next stop on the nationwide tour is Detroit in late March. I know I'm wearing a T-shirt that reads "Detroit" in my website photo, but that's for the street cred – I've never actually been there. I bought this great autobiography in the airport by Brett Pitman Hart (sp?) – it had the jacket cover on it but that was getting ripped so I took it off, and I remember sitting in her hotel with this big pink book thinking, I'm glad this woman does everything on foot, because I don't know where the hell anything is around here.

She's an athlete so she doesn't usually take any form of transportation; her meetings are always within walking distance of wherever she's staying, and so are the restaurants that she visits, the hot spots, what have you. This particular day I was in the lobby waiting for her, and she comes down and hops in a cab. So, I'm like…fuck. It wasn't like the movies where the next cab pulls up, and I say: Follow that cab! Here I am walking out with this big pink book, that's as thick as the Bible, and I've got to hoof it. In her honor I tried to get a pretty good pace going, but I ended up having to sprint about twelve blocks…we're maneuvering through city traffic, and I'm trying to gauge the lights. Her cab's behind me and I'm looking back, like I would tailing someone in a car. The light's going from green to yellow, she's taking a right, there's a lot of stop and start, and I can't believe she doesn't notice me. Does she not notice some white dude running through the streets of Detroit with a big pink book under his arm – like O.J. Simpson, sprinting through the airport? It's like I'm carrying this big sign that says, "Hello! I'm following you!"

The truth is, she doesn't notice me because she's not guilty of anything. She doesn't have anything on her conscience. I followed her to six U.S. cities in eighteen months and I never found anything. Never! You know, I think I'm somewhat of a good looking guy. She won't even fucking look at me! I've been in her face 1,000 times. I can't help but wonder if she ever thinks, This is the same guy that I've seen all over the country… Obviously it's not conscious, because she would freak out pretty badly if she realized she's being tailed by a professional stalker. But does it ever cross her mind, just once, "My God, why does that guy look so familiar???"

Each time I report back to Andrew that his wife isn't cheating, he presses me more and more. Am I sure I saw her turn in for the night? Do I know where she went before breakfast? Dude, she ran a marathon yesterday. I saw here at 7:30am this morning eating a bran muffin. I highly doubt she met her lover any earlier than that. Still he keeps on, indulging in his self-torture as I call it, another theme of this book. He isn't satisfied with 100 instances of everything being okay or as it should be, he needs to find that one instance where things might be a little off and then investigate it... or have me investigate it for him. He wants to know, he has to find out – even if there's nothing – because he's afraid of the unknown. Everything is driven by the fact that he's a fear-based personality. He's afraid that if his wife ever did leave him, that he wouldn't be able to live his life.

So what is his problem? I'm not a psychologist, but obviously he's paranoid. He's afraid of losing her, so he goes to these extremes. We're all afraid on some level. I'm afraid of losing my wife, but I don't ratchet it up and have her and her girlfriends followed, when I could basically do it for free. I don't, because there's got to be some degree of trust; I've never used my skills or connections – I swear on my kids – ever, in any relationship. But I can't sit here and say to you that I don't get insecure. I can relate to Andrew in a way, he's just the guy who will cross over that threshold, maybe because he has the financial means to do it.

I say Andrew's like a lot of guys, but it's not true of all of us. Take my friend, Frank, for example…he doesn't give a shit. He's got that laid back personality. If his girlfriend cheats, she cheats. He doesn't get upset, he doesn't get jealous. But if you've got a type-A personality, like me, we do get insecure, we do get jealous. We're tempted to read our partner's emails… to listen in to their phone conversations… to see who they've been texting… But if we do indulge in a little spying, how many times does our subject turn out to be innocent before we let it go? Before we say, Okay, enough is enough. She's not cheating. Or is it just the act of spying in that creates the paranoia, in which case…

In which case I have to reconsider whether I want to be a part of this any longer. I used to compare being a P.I. to being a stripper at times: you're looking at your clients, and you're fucking hating them, but you know that you have to take their money. It's your job. Some of my clients make me want to puke when I think of the things they want done, but I do it – and I try not to complain about it. I simply provide them the service they are looking for.

But through the years, and most importantly through my relationship with my wife Stephanie, I've grown. How did I end up in a normal relationship, anyway? I don't want to be that guy who has to know every single thing that his wife's doing every day. I don't want to control her, or have her feel like she has to report back to me constantly, "Here I am, honey. Here I am, honey. Here I am, honey." And I don't really want to be a part of taking some guy's money who just can't control himself, but has to call me when I'm out on a job constantly to get some weird, voyeuristic pleasure in knowing exactly what his wife is up to at any given moment.

The last time I ever followed his wife was in New Orleans. She ran the marathon and then she went to the Mardi Gras parade. I've got Andrew texting me over and over and over and over and over. What's she doing now? What's she doing now? At the exact moment of one of his texts she was on Bourbon Street and somebody put a rubber penis in her hand. I texted him, "She's holding a penis." So of course he called me right away!

I pushed "ignore" when I saw his number, and I took a picture of his wife and the dildo-looking thing instead. She's wearing this cute, embarrassed expression, and I texted the photo to him. Then I called him back to personally deliver the news: Your wife is not cheating on you. This rubber penis is as far as it goes, and this is as far as I go, too. I'm not doing this anymore. It doesn't matter how much you pay me. You've got a problem, and I hope someday, bro, you figure it out.

Coda

I get calls all the time from people who need counseling, and I'm free with my advice – regardless of whether or not the individual on the other end of the phone is a client, or might turn into one.

Some guy from Michigan might call, for example, and say that his wife is coming into Boston on the 4th of July. He has her itinerary, and he wants her followed. When I explain to him that this is the most chaotic day of the year in our neck of the woods and that he's going to need at least two or three different agents, it's too expensive for him – so I end up just talking to him for half an hour instead.

I got a call a few months ago from a woman, Donna, who lives in Georgia. She thinks her husband might be cheating on her. I wanted to know what the connection to Massachusetts is, is he up here on business?

"No," she says, "you just look like a nice guy. I saw your picture on the website and I just want some advice."

She goes into the whole story about the signs of him cheating, and then she tells me that he's kicking the shit out of her. He's beating her up and they have kids.

In subsequent phone calls I know I'm dealing with battered woman syndrome; I'm trying to tell her that cheating is irrelevant at this point, get out of the marriage to protect you and your kids. Call the police.

"Well, I already have a restraining order," she tells me, "If I call again he'll be arrested, and I love him.

"Just tell me: is hitting people a sign of cheating?" That's all she wants to know.

I tell her, "No, ma'am. Talking on your cell phone, staying out late, changing your cologne – those are signs of cheating. Domestic abuse isn't a sign of anything else. It's a sign of getting your ass kicked."

I was finally able to convince her, a tornado isn't a sign of a windy day. It's a fucking tornado. Just a couple of days ago I got a call from her – she and her kids have moved out, and they're thinking about coming up to New England for vacation. You know, see the birthplace of liberty and all that crap. I told her I was really happy for her, but that she should save her money – she had her own liberty now, and nothing could ever be sweeter than that.

About the Author

Mark W. Chauppetta is a dedicated father and husband who started his professional career in 1990 with the Massachusetts Department of Corrections. After a few years of working the graveyard shift, shining his boots, and listening to head strong superiors he grew tired of the grey light of prison, and decided to pack his bags for sunny California. He originally intended to pursue his lifelong dream of an acting career, but after a year of classes, auditions and serving wheat grass to lotus-eaters he knew he needed something with a little more meat. Mark became a PI apprentice under his now good friend and mentor, Douglas Florence. After a year of random and instructive capers, Mark moved back east opening up MWC Investigations in Brockton, Ma, which later evolved in On the Mark Investigations. Mark's reputation as a hard-nosed PI who isn't afraid to walk that fine line to get results is complemented by his passionate advocacy for Duchenne's Muscular Dystrophy which struck his twin sons. Most recently, Mark produced an award winning documentary, *A Father's Fight*, which chronicles his experience as a mixed martial arts fighter in support of a cure of this terrible disease.

5774131R0

Made in the USA
Charleston, SC
01 August 2010